EXPLORING THE ANCIENT
AND MEDIEVAL WORLDS

The Fall of Rome and the Rise of Constantinople

Zachary Anderson

Cavendish Square

New York

Published in 2016 by Cavendish Square Publishing, LLC
243 5th Avenue, Suite 136, New York, NY 10016

Cataloging-in-Publication Data

Anderson, Zachary.
The fall of Rome and the rise of Constantinople / by Zachary Anderson.
p. cm. — (Exploring the ancient and medieval worlds)
Includes index.
ISBN 978-1-50260-574-0 (hardcover) ISBN 978-1-50260-575-7 (ebook)
1. Rome — History — Empire, 284 - 476 — Juvenile literature 2. Rome — History — Germanic Invasions, 3rd - 6th centuries — Juvenile literature. 3. Rome — Civilization — Juvenile literature. I. Anderson, Zachary. II. Title.
DG311.A588 2016
937'.06—d23

Editorial Director: David McNamara
Editor: Andrew Coddington
Copy Editor: Regina Murrell
Art Director: Jeff Talbot
Designer: Joseph Macri
Senior Production Manager: Jennifer Ryder-Talbot
Production Editor: Renni Johnson
Photo Research: J8 Media

Printed in the United States of America

Contents

The Roman emperor Hadrian built this wall in 122 CE at the border between Rome's territories in Britain and Scotland, which was controlled by the barbarian Picts.

CHAPTER ONE

On the Borders of the Empire

By the early second century CE, the Roman Empire contained all of the territories around the Mediterranean and large parts of Europe and the Near East. While some of the peoples lived at the edges of the empire, others were valued trading partners.

The Roman Empire reached its greatest extent during the reign of the emperor Trajan, who ruled between 98 and 117 CE. By the time of Trajan's death, the empire stretched from the borders of Scotland in the northwest to the upper Nile in the southeast. While the Romans ruled confidently over the territories they had conquered and annexed, they knew comparatively little about the regions beyond their borders. The little information that did reach the Romans suggested that this hinterland was a hostile and threatening place. The tribes that inhabited the areas around the edges of the empire often harassed the Roman frontier, which had to be permanently garrisoned to keep out the enemy.

European Tribes

Although a small number of important provinces were added in the years that followed, the broad extent of the Roman Empire had been established by the time of the death of the emperor Augustus in 14 CE. Augustus had suggested that his successors should not attempt to extend the empire further, and the emperors of the first century CE generally followed this advice. In Europe, the Rhine and Danube rivers were regarded as natural boundaries, and the Romans rarely tried to conquer the areas beyond them. Most emperors did not want the financial burden of an expensive military campaign; they were also not keen to allow their generals to gain personal glory from such conquests.

Generally, the Romans had only scant knowledge of the tribes of northern Europe beyond the Roman frontier. One exception to this rule was the Roman historian Tacitus (circa 56–120 CE). Tacitus thought highly of the Germanic tribes and believed they exhibited some of the ancient Roman virtues, such as simplicity of lifestyle, personal fidelity, and great bravery. According to Tacitus, the Germans were as yet unspoiled by the decadence of the civilized world.

Tacitus's view of German life was far removed from reality, however. Most groups lived in great poverty and were constantly involved in local wars. They elected a leader or king only in times of great emergency, when a warrior was lifted on a shield in a meeting of

The Seleucid Dynasty

The Seleucid dynasty was founded in the late fourth century CE by Seleucus I, a former general in the army of Alexander the Great. By the time of his death in 281 BCE, Seleucus had succeeded in conquering Anatolia, Babylonia, Assyria, Parthia, Bactria, and a number of other areas of Asia that had formerly been part of the Macedonian Empire. However, over the next half century, the dynasty suffered from constant disputes over the succession, which weakened the empire to such an extent that it lost eastern Iran and the greater part of Anatolia. In 223 BCE, a new, energetic king, Antiochus III, came to the throne. He made determined efforts to recover control of the provinces in the east and to expand his territory in the west. However, when he came up against the power of Rome, he was driven back and defeated in 190 BCE.

Antiochus was succeeded by Seleucus IV, who inherited an empire that stretched from east of the Persian Gulf to Syria and Phoenicia in the west. By 140 BCE, however, the whole region east of Syria had fallen to the Parthians. Pompey's annexation of Syria in 63 BCE brought the Seleucid Empire to an end.

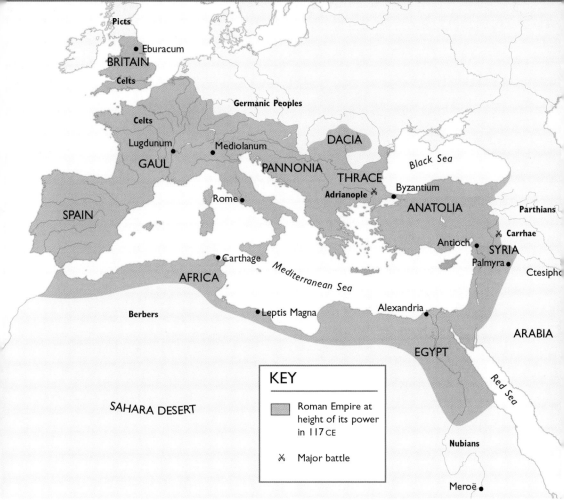

free men. The power of these leaders depended largely on their success in battle. Those who led their people into the rich border territories of the Romans seem to have acquired enormous prestige, eventually making their kingships hereditary.

The Germanic tribes of central-northern Europe were migrants and had displaced the Celts, who had inhabited the territory previously. The **Celts** were spread all over western Europe, including Gaul and the northern Roman province of Britain. Here, in the extreme north, in a region called Caledonia (present-day Scotland) lived a warlike people known to the Romans as the **Picts**. Around 122 CE, the emperor **Hadrian** built a fortified wall across the country to keep the Picts out. However, the Romans never completely managed to stop the Picts from raiding south of the wall.

These ruins stand in the city of Ctesiphon, the capital of the Parthian Empire. This palace was built between the third and sixth centuries CE by the Persian successors of the Parthians.

The Eastern Border

On its eastern border, the Roman Empire rarely extended beyond the Euphrates River into **Mesopotamia**. On the other side of the river lay the territory of the **Parthians**. Divided into small, patriarchal groups, the Parthians had lived for centuries in what is now northeastern Iran. They lived peacefully under the Persian and the early Seleucid kings (see sidebar, page 6) until around 250 BCE, when a neighboring people, the **Bactrians**, rebelled against their Seleucid overlords. Soon afterward, the Parthian king Arsaces succeeded in gaining independence from the Seleucids and extending his territory to the southwest.

Over the next two hundred years, the Parthians profited from the weakening of the Seleucid Empire by increasing their own power. Eventually, the Parthians controlled all of ancient Persia and Mesopotamia. In 63 BCE, when Pompey the Great created the Roman province of Syria out of the remnants of the Seleucid Empire, the Parthians became Rome's neighbors and rivals. They remained so for the next three hundred years.

Between 114 and 117 CE, the Roman emperor Trajan mounted a huge expedition to the east and succeeded in conquering the whole of Mesopotamia. In the process, he destroyed the Parthian capital **Ctesiphon**. Trajan died before he could consolidate his gains, however, and his successor, the emperor Hadrian, gave up Mesopotamia and made peace with the Parthians. Toward the end of the second century CE, the Parthians suffered another heavy defeat at the hands of the Romans, when the emperor Septimus Severus annexed the north of Mesopotamia to the Roman Empire, again reducing Ctesiphon to ruins.

The Parthians never really recovered from these blows, largely due to the weak political organization of their empire. In spirit, they had always remained a nomadic people and did not feel permanently rooted in the lands of Mesopotamia and Persia. Around 230 CE, their empire finally collapsed when Persians from the south rebelled against Parthian rule. The Parthian dynasty was replaced by a new family of Persian rulers, called the Sassanid dynasty. Intent on restoring the old Persian Empire, the **Sassanids** continued the centuries-old war against Rome with renewed energy, but the decades of strife that followed only led to the chronic weakening of both empires.

These pyramids are located at Meroë, the ancient capital of Nubia, a kingdom that lay to the south of Egypt.

Arabian Wealth

For centuries, the wealthy merchant cities of southern Arabia occupied a pivotal position between the east and the west. The cities' inhabitants owed their prosperity to the trade in Indian spices and their own desert products, such as incense. Particularly prosperous was the city of Aden. Merchants from Egypt and Syria, with whom it traded, called the area around the city "Happy Arabia" because of its extensive irrigation works that allowed it to grow crops in a region that was otherwise covered in desert.

Eventually, in the second century BCE, the Egyptians discovered the secret of the Arabs' maritime trade with India. The monsoon winds blew across the Indian Ocean in one direction for six months of the year and in the reverse direction for the other six months. Ships could take advantage of the change of wind direction and sail back and forth across the vast ocean. Once this secret was out, the inhabitants of southern Arabia lost their monopoly on Indian trade. Southern Arabia retained its importance only as a supplier of incense, which was transported north by caravan via the old trading center of Mecca. As Arabia declined, the irrigation works around Aden fell into disuse. By the Middle Ages, the area was little different from the rest of the barren peninsula.

Egypt, Arabia, and Africa

When Augustus defeated the Egyptian queen Cleopatra at the Battle of Actium in 31 BCE, he moved swiftly to annex the whole of Egypt as a Roman province. By doing so, he inherited the Egyptians' rivalry with the Nubians, a warlike desert people who inhabited part of what is present-day Sudan. The Nubians had been intermittent enemies of the Egyptians for centuries. By Augustus's time, they had become formidable opponents. The Nubian Empire, centered around the city of Meroë, shared many cultural elements with that of the ancient Egyptian pharaohs. At the time of the Roman annexation, the Nubian queen was constantly harassing the Egyptian border, sending warrior bands to raid southern Egypt.

Because Rome depended on grain supplies from Egypt, Augustus sent an expeditionary force to defeat the Nubians. The legions penetrated Nubia almost as far as Meroë. The Romans set up a garrison in the region to maintain control over this southernmost outpost of the empire. Nevertheless, Roman influence in Nubia remained minimal.

At the same time that he mounted the expedition against the Nubians, Augustus sent an army into Arabia. The campaign was a disaster, however. A six-month march through the desert claimed

These Roman ruins stand in the Tunisian city of Dougga. Like much of Northern Africa, Dougga came under Roman control in the second century BCE.

many lives, and the survivors had to turn back before they could achieve their goals.

On the coast of northern Africa, the Romans had conquered and destroyed Carthage in the second century BCE. The lands of the Carthaginian Empire had subsequently been annexed as the Roman province of Africa. Roman power never extended far into the hinterland, however. Like the Carthaginians before them, the Romans were satisfied with the fertile regions on the African coast. The Sahara Desert, just south of the coastal rim, was a formidable barrier that effectively put a stop to further expansion.

The Romans maintained good relations with the nomadic Berber people who inhabited the region of present-day Morocco and Algeria. Until the third century CE, when unrest spread throughout the empire, there was little to disturb the peaceful life of the Romans living in the rich coastal areas of northern Africa. The many ruins of Roman villas and cities in the region are a testament to its prosperity.

Rome's Allies

During the time of the Roman republic, the **foederati** (designated allies) were tribes who were bound by treaty to the Romans yet did not form official Roman colonies. They were allowed to maintain their own institutions and legal and state systems, but they had to supply soldiers for the Roman army on demand.

In the third century CE, the empire was riddled with internal strife, and numerous tribes living on the borders exploited the situation by invading the Roman provinces. Although the invaders were "often driven back, the victories were never conclusive. Eventually, the Romans decided to allow the invading tribes to settle in the empire on the condition that they accepted Roman authority and provided troops to augment the army. This move brought peace to the borders, and the new settlers acted as buffers against future attacks.

India and China

For several centuries, India was separated from the Roman Empire by the land of the Parthians. Egypt, however, engaged in maritime trade with India from the late second century BCE onward, and once Egypt became a Roman province in 30 BCE, trade between Rome and India grew. Many Roman coins have been found on the coasts of India, suggesting that trading contacts were frequent. India offered spices such as cinnamon and nutmeg, plus pearls, ivory, textiles, and exotic animals. These goods were traded for Alexandrian glass, bronze kitchenware, and minted gold and silver coins. Imports from India were always luxury items, which were eagerly sought after by wealthy, upper-class Roman citizens.

All that the Romans knew about China was that it lay far to the east and produced silk. Toward the end of the second century BCE, the Chinese had established an overland trading route that would carry their silk to the west, where it found ready buyers. A stream of merchants with pack animals moved steadily from China to the foot of the Pamir Mountains, where their goods were transferred to the hands of Persian and Syrian merchants, who continued the journey to the west. This was the famous **Silk Road**, which remained the only regular link between China and the west until the Middle Ages.

This relief is a detail from the Ludovisi Battle sarcophagus, dating to the third century CE, which depicts scenes from a battle between Romans and Germans. Here, a Roman soldier intimidates a German prisoner whose hands are bound.

CHAPTER TWO

Rome's Decline

The rise of the emperor Commodus to the throne in 180 CE ushered in an unstable period of Roman history. The following century saw a succession of short-reigning emperors, many of whom had to contend with rival claimants.

By the late second century CE, cracks had begun to appear in the Roman Empire. Commerce and industry were in decline, bringing urban decay and political chaos. Agriculture, too, was deteriorating, leading to poverty and unrest in the once-flourishing provinces. Renewed invasions, civil war, and economic ruin would all be factors in the eventual collapse of the empire.

Many of these problems were rooted in the era of the Antonine emperors, although that period itself had seemed to be one of great prosperity. For nearly one hundred years, each emperor had nominated a non-relative as his successor. This system had generally proved to be successful. The years of good government ended, however, when **Marcus Aurelius** nominated his young son, Commodus, to be emperor.

The Reign of Commodus

Commodus was nominally made co-emperor at age sixteen. He inherited the empire three and a half years later in 180 CE. Marcus Aurelius's intention had been to train Commodus for the position, but the young man seems to have paid little attention to his lessons. Instead, he was interested only in seeking his own pleasure. Once

Commodus inherited the crown, he became extremely paranoid; he lived in constant fear for his life and summarily executed anyone he suspected of plotting against him. He handed out the work of the empire to a collection of his favorites, leaving himself free to enjoy the delights of Rome. Commodus ignored his father's foreign policy, including plans to expand the empire into central Europe. The frontiers held only because of the capable administration of the provincial governors and the settlement arrangements that Aurelius had made with the tribes on the Danube.

The emperor's particular hobby was gladiatorial combat. Commodus loved to watch it and, even more, to take part in it. He would perform in the amphitheater dressed as Hercules, shooting or clubbing to death wild animals. He made the senate officially recognize him as a god as a reward for these achievements. Such behavior earned him many enemies among the upper classes, and his disastrous rule was brought to an end prematurely in 192 CE, when conspirators bribed his regular wrestling partner to strangle him. On Commodus's death, the senate declared him *damnatio memoriae*, meaning that his reign was expunged from official records.

Buying the Throne

The assassins of Commodus put forward the sixty-six-year-old Helvius Pertinax, the prefect of Rome, as a candidate for emperor, and he was accepted by the senate. Pertinax made a good start to his reign when he attempted to restore the financial stability of the state by curbing expenditure. He had no personal wealth, however, and he incurred the wrath of the **Praetorian Guard** because of his inability to pay them the tribute that was customary on an emperor's accession. They murdered him in 193 CE.

Titus Flavius Sulpicianus, Pertinax's father-in-law and a wealthy senator, then offered the Praetorians twenty thousand sesterces each for the throne. His colleague, the aging but even more wealthy Didius Julianus, outbid him, offering each Praetorian twenty-five thousand sesterces. The soldiers accepted the offer and escorted Julianus to the senate, which could do nothing but confirm his nomination. The principate had become a commodity to be bought and sold.

The Severan Dynasty

When news of the "sale" of the principate reached the provinces, three powerful armies challenged the authority of Julianus, beginning the civil war of 193 CE. The army nearest to Rome was that situated on the Danube River, and it declared its commander, Septimius Severus, emperor in May. Severus entered Rome without opposition. The senate accepted him and, at the same time, condemned Julianus to death.

In Syria, the legate Pescennius Niger had been nominated as emperor by his troops, while in Britain, Clodius Albinus was nominated by his. In an attempt to neutralize part of the opposition, Severus gave Albinus the title of Caesar, which was now used to designate the heir apparent to the

Septimus Severus, ruled 193–211 CE

throne. This move made Albinus an ally, temporarily, at least. Then, in a brilliant campaign, Severus marched on Niger, dislodging him from his new conquests near the Black Sea and finally defeating and killing him in 194 CE.

Two years later, Albinus proclaimed himself Augustus, a title that implied a share in imperial power. He proceeded to invade Gaul, where he met the army of Severus at **Lugdunum** (present-day Lyon, France) in 197 CE. In a hard-fought battle, Severus proved victorious. Albinus was killed, leaving Severus as the undisputed emperor.

Severus's reign ushered in the short-lived dynasty of the Severi. The Severan emperors imposed what has been called a military monarchy on the Roman Empire. The emperor dominated both the army and the senate and dictated all new legislation. Severus himself had been born into an aristocratic provincial family in the city of Leptis Magna, near Tripoli in northern Africa, and had held both political offices and military command. In 180 CE, he had married Julia Domna, whose father was ruler of the Syrian city of Emesa and high priest in the temple of Baal (see sidebar, page 23). Julia was to exert great influence on her husband and even rule the empire while he was at war.

Severus sought to exploit the popularity of the Antonine emperors by declaring himself the adopted son of Marcus Aurelius. He also named his eldest son, later to be known as Caracalla, Marcus Aurelius. However, the policies Severus pursued were quite different from those of his popular predecessors. His focus was provincial rather than aristocratic, and he never forgot that he owed his position to the army of the Danube. Severus established a new social order dominated by equestrians (members of the mercantile middle class) and opened both military and civilian careers to the lower classes. As for his faithful Danube army, he placed his elite officers in charge of the Praetorian Guard and enrolled three new legions under equestrian command. He also added thousand-soldier auxiliary units to both the infantry and the cavalry.

The Severan revolution extended throughout the administration. Severus reduced the privileges of the peoples of the Italian Peninsula and increased those of easterners and Africans, recruiting the latter to government posts for the first time. Severus had a keen interest in the processes of the law, and he appointed a famous jurist, Papinian, as Praetorian prefect and commissioned him to systemize the law, a move that gave Severus the opportunity to involve his office in the administration of justice.

Severus proved himself an energetic campaigner in foreign affairs. In the east, the Parthians had supported Niger in the civil war, and after defeating his rival claimant, Severus invaded Mesopotamia. However, he was soon called away to deal with Albinus in the west and had to conclude a hasty peace with the Parthians. In the summer of 197 CE, Severus returned to the east to punish the Parthian king, who had attacked the Roman frontier. Severus defeated the Parthians and annexed Mesopotamia as a new province. On his return to Rome, Severus built a triumphal arch in the Forum Romanum to glorify his success against the Parthians.

Severus's other main campaign took place in Britain, where tribes from Scotland had penetrated as far south as **Eboracum** (present-day York). Although the governor had succeeded in bribing them to return north of Hadrian's Wall, Severus embarked on a punitive expedition in 208 CE. While extensive repairs were carried out to the wall, which had been badly damaged during the Picts' invasion, Severus and his sons conducted raids on the aggressive northerners. Although they failed to bring the invaders to battle, the Roman show of strength seems to have had an effect; there were no more incursions for almost a hundred years. Severus fell ill during this campaign and died at Eburacum in 211 CE.

Caracalla

Severus had intended that his two sons, then in their early twenties, should rule jointly on his death. However, this arrangement did not suit the elder son, Caracalla. Within a year of his father's death, Caracalla had arranged for his younger brother, Geta, to be assassinated. Geta died in the arms of their mother, Julia Domna.

Caracalla considered himself to be a god and believed that his father had ascended to the sun on his death. Caracalla's reign was characterized by extravagance, debauchery, and cruelty. However, he continued the egalitarian social policies and judicial and legislative changes begun by his father. In 212 CE, Caracalla conferred Roman citizenship on all free inhabitants of the empire so that, for the first time, everyone in the empire had equal status. Because certain taxes were paid only by Romans, this move may have been partially motivated by financial considerations.

Caracalla spent freely. He increased the pay of the ordinary soldiers, in spite of a shrinking treasury, and embarked on an extensive building program, including completing the great public baths begun by his father. These baths became known as the Baths of Caracalla. To help cover the costs of all the projects, Caracalla increased the taxes on senators and doubled the inheritance tax and emancipation tax (the tax paid by manumitted or freed slaves). He also debased the coinage by introducing a new silver coin, the antoninianus, which had a face value of two denarii, although it weighed considerably less than one denarius.

Adopting Alexander the Great as his model, Caracalla began an ambitious campaign in the east. However, in 217 CE, while his army was on the march in Mesopotamia, Caracalla was murdered by a group of officers led by the Praetorian prefect Marcus Opellius Macrinus.

The Rise of Macrinus

Unaware of Macrinus's complicity in the death of their commander, Caracalla's soldiers hailed him as emperor. The senate reluctantly confirmed this appointment. Macrinus was a member of the equestrian order, and was the first *eques* to be made emperor. In his short reign, Macrinus succeeded in completing Caracalla's objective of bringing the whole of Mesopotamia under Roman rule. However, he only managed to do so by paying the Parthians substantial sums of money to give up their claims. In a bid to increase his popularity with the Roman people, Macrinus reduced the military budget and canceled the taxes his predecessor had implemented.

In Syria, a plot was launched to put the grandnephew of Julia Domna (the late widow of Severus) on the throne. This young man, only fourteen years old at the time, was called Bassianus, and he was a chief priest of Baal, the local sun god. The legions in Syria acclaimed him as emperor (having been liberally bribed to do so). The armies of the two rival claimants met in battle near Antioch in 218 CE. The forces of Macrinus were defeated. The emperor himself fled and was later killed.

Elagabalus: The Exotic Emperor

The new emperor, Bassianus, had been brought up in a temple to the Syrian sun god, Baal. He was therefore known as El-a-Gabal, the son of Baal, a name that the Romans changed to Elagabalus. Presented to the senate as the illegitimate son of Caracalla, he also took the name Marcus Aurelius Antoninus.

Elagabalus quickly made himself extremely unpopular with the Roman populace because of his extravagance and outrageous behavior. He appeared in the palace dressed as the high priest of Baal and made it clear that he hoped to impose the worship of Baal on the whole empire. Elagabalus built a temple dedicated to his god in

The emperor Elagabalus tried to impose the worship of the Syrian sun god Baal (pictured above).

Rome and spent enormous sums of money on religious ceremonies and sacrifices to Baal. Many of Elagabalus's acts seemed sacrilegious to the Romans. For example, when he ordered an ancient statue of the virgin goddess Vesta to be dragged to the temple of Baal, there was a huge outcry.

Elagabalus also outraged Rome with his sexual behavior. He engaged in openly homosexual relationships (in particular, one with his charioteer Hierocles), and stories of his orgies spread throughout the city. Animosity toward Elagabalus intensified. After four years, the Romans had had enough. The Praetorian Guard murdered him and threw his body in the Tiber. His cousin, Severus Alexander, was installed in his place.

Severus Alexander: The Boy Emperor

Severus Alexander came to the throne in 222 CE, when he was only fourteen years old. He was the son of Julia Mamaea, the niece of Julia Domna. Alexander had a very different character from that of his immediate predecessor. Alexander was serious and docile, and he had a high regard for the office of emperor. He ruled with the help of his mother, and for much of the first decade of his reign, the empire enjoyed a period of internal peace. The *consilium principis* (the emperor's imperial council, on which lawyers and senators sat) was reorganized and regained its former influence, thereby reinforcing the civilian element of government at the expense of the military.

However, the peaceful times did not last. Around 230 CE, trouble broke out in the east, where the Persians (who had overrun and defeated the Parthians) attacked Mesopotamia in an attempt to win back some of their long-lost territories. Although poorly suited to the role of warrior, the emperor saw it as his duty to go into battle. After a defensive war in the east, the princeps traveled to the Rhine, where there were also threats of invasion. There, in 235 CE, during a riot among the troops in Moguntiacum (present-day Mainz), Alexander was killed. His death brought the **Severan dynasty** to an end.

The Soldier Emperors

The riot in which Alexander was killed had been instigated by Maximinus, an uneducated provincial soldier from Thrace. Maximinus was immediately proclaimed emperor by his troops, and his short reign ushered in half a century of disastrous civil anarchy, during which time no fewer that twenty-six emperors were appointed.

Although illiterate, Maximinus was an experienced and competent soldier. He was barely recognized as princeps in the empire when, almost immediately, he had to crush two rebellions. When Germans attacked the Rhine border, he quickly restored order there with a victory in 235 CE. In the provinces along the Danube River, trouble was fomented by the **Goths**, a Germanic people from the coast of the Baltic. These tribes dared to challenge the might of the Roman Empire, plundering Greece and pillaging ships in the Black Sea. Here again, Maximinus eventually managed to reassert the supremacy of Rome.

The God Baal

Baal was a very ancient fertility god, worshipped by the Canaanites and Phoenicians as early as 3000 BCE. He was originally believed to be a storm god who brought the rain that was essential for growing crops. Many temples were dedicated to Baal. A number of rituals were carried out to placate him, and some of them may have involved human sacrifice.

However, the word *baal* simply meant "lord." Consequently, many other gods in eastern religions came to be called Baal, which explains why the sun god worshipped in Syria in the second century CE was also referred to as Baal. This sun god, whose name was El-Gabal, was considered to be the lord of the universe. He was often depicted standing beside an eagle, the symbol of divine authority. In Syria, the center of the sun cult was located in the holy city of Emesa, where the emperor Severus's wife, Julia Domna, had been born to the high priest of El-Gabal. When her grandnephew became emperor, he took the name Elagabalus (son of El-Gabal). He later shocked the Romans with his adherence to the rites of the sun god, reportedly dressing up as the high priest of the god and leading orgiastic processions through the streets of Rome.

Despite these successes, Maximinus had not endeared himself to the senate. A simple soldier, he had no time for an educated elite and did not care who knew it. In 238 CE, a group of disgruntled landowners in northern Africa joined with the senate in a rebellion against the emperor. The insurgents proclaimed Gordian I, the proconsul of Africa, as the new emperor; he, in turn, nominated his son, Gordian II, as his successor. However, within weeks, both Gordians were dead, killed in a conflict with Capelianus, a Numidian governor loyal to Maximinus. Maximinus then marched on Rome, but he was killed by his own army before he could set foot in the city. The response of the senate was to place Gordian III (the grandson of Gordian I) on the throne.

Only thirteen years old when he became emperor, Gordian III held power for five years, during which time the Persians invaded

Mesopotamia and Syria, reaching as far as Antioch. On campaign against the Persians, Gordian was murdered in 244 CE by Philip the Arabian, an Arab who had made a career in the Roman army. Philip made peace with the Persians by ceding part of the empire to them and paying a cash tribute. He also secured victories over the German tribes in 246 CE and the **Carpi** in **Dacia** the following year. His fabulous victory celebrations in Rome coincided with the city's one-thousandth anniversary. The Roman people wanted to believe that a period of peace and prosperity had begun. However, events proved that this was not to be the case.

Another pretender, an officer called **Decius**, who commanded the troops in Dacia, invaded Italy and fought Philip at a battle near Verona in 249 CE. Philip and his young son were killed, and Decius entered Rome in triumph. As the new princeps, Decius attempted to eradicate the eastern religions that had infiltrated the empire, including the imperial residence. These religions included Christianity, and Decius seized all church property and demanded a declaration of loyalty from his subjects, compelling them to make sacrifices to the gods of state in front of official witnesses. Many Christians refused to comply and died for their convictions.

Decius's attack was a heavy blow for the Christian community. Since the time of Marcus Aurelius's rule in the late second century CE, Christians had generally been left in peace. Some had won converts in the highest Roman circles. Now, many of these new believers renounced their faith rather than die as martyrs.

When, in his bid for the principate, Decius left Dacia, the region around it became vulnerable to attack. In 251 CE, a tribe known as the Goths crossed the Danube and invaded Roman territory. Decius hurried back to Dacia to confront them. However, he walked into an ambush. Decius was killed, and his army was totally destroyed.

Valerian and Gallienus

After a series of short-lived emperors, two Roman senators, father and son, began to reign jointly in 253 CE. The father, Valerian, had great personal integrity, but his qualities were not enough to restore the might of Rome. The anarchy of the previous few years had resulted in a crumbling border, and the forces stationed there could no longer repel the onslaughts of the surrounding tribes. While his son Gallienus attempted to hold the line on the Rhine, the Danube, and in Spain, Valerian confronted the Persian king Shapur I in the east. In 258 CE, Valerian was taken prisoner by the Persians. He died in captivity two years later—an unprecedented humiliation for a Roman princeps.

Gallienus was left to rule on his own. He faced formidable difficulties and did not have sufficient forces to deal with them. The borders of the empire needed constant defense, and rival kingdoms were set up in Gaul and in Palmyra (see sidebar, page 26–27). To ensure that his army operated at maximum efficiency, he only appointed equites to positions of high military command, a move that antagonized the senate.

Gallienus was an educated man and had a particular interest in Greek culture. He was an adherent to the ancient Greek cult of **Demeter**. However, he was tolerant of all sects and halted the persecution of Christians. These acts made him extremely unpopular among the traditionalists of the Roman elite.

After a number of campaign victories on the Rhine and the Danube, Gallienus found his resources stretched too thin to combat the governments in Gaul and Palmyra. When he returned to Italy to

Government in Exile

In 259 CE, the legions in Gaul appointed their commander, Marcus Postumus, as princeps. Recognized in Gaul, and later in Spain and Britain, Postumus set up in present-day Trier what might be called a "government in exile," complete with a senate and annually elected consuls. He issued his own coins and maintained his own Praetorian Guard. His vast rival empire remained stable for eight years, during which time he defended the Rhine border against incursions by the Germanic tribes. Eventually, Postumus was killed by his own soldiers. He was replaced by Tetricus, the governor of **Aquitania**. Tetricus was defeated by the emperor Aurelian in 274 CE, bringing the rebel state to an end.

The Roman governor of Palmyra, Odaenathus, successfully broke ties with the empire, ruling the city until his assassination in 268 CE.

The Rogue Kingdom
of Palmyra

After around 260 CE, the prosperous desert city of Palmyra in Syria became increasingly powerful under the rule of Odaenathus, the Roman governor appointed by Gallienus to maintain law and order and keep the Persians at bay. The people of Syria organized their own guerrilla bands to assist Odaenathus, who ultimately defeated the Persians near Carrhae.

Odaenathus began to call himself the king of Palmyra. However, he never attempted to take over as emperor, nominally recognizing the authority in Rome. He proved to be a gifted ruler, and Gallienus could do nothing but offer his approval, first with the title Imperator and later with Inspector of All the East.

When Odaenathus was murdered around 268 CE, his widow, Zenobia, immediately took control. She bestowed all of Odaenathus's titles on her infant son, Vaballathus, and set up an independent eastern monarchy in the Persian style. At that time, the emperors in Rome were fully occupied repelling barbarian invasions in Europe, so Zenobia embarked on a campaign to expand her kingdom. In 269 CE, she invaded Egypt, deposed and killed the Roman prefect governing the country, and had herself declared queen. Zenobia then conquered Anatolia, Syria, Palestine, and Lebanon.

Once the Roman emperor Aurelian had successfully dealt with his rivals in Europe, he turned his attentions to the east. Aurelian recovered Rome's former provinces with relative ease and defeated Zenobia in battle at Immae and Emesa. She was later captured and taken to Rome as a captive. Aurelian showed mercy on the former queen and spared her life. Zenobia later married a Roman senator.

The Aurelian Wall, completed in 275 CE, was built to protect Rome from barbarian invasion.

confront one of his generals, Aureolus, who was attempting to usurp the throne, Gallienus was murdered by his own officers in Mediolanum in 268 CE.

The Illyrian Emperors

After the assassination of Gallienus, the army appointed an **Illyrian**, Claudius II, as their emperor. Almost immediately, he had to face a serious invasion by the Goths, who were determined to occupy the Balkan Peninsula. In a brilliant campaign, Claudius inflicted a savage defeat on the invading tribes, putting an end to the Gothic menace for the next one hundred years. However, his reign was cut short when he died of the plague in 270 CE.

Claudius was succeeded by several more Illyrian emperors, all of whom tried energetically to restore stability to the empire. The first of them was Aurelian, who ruled from 270 to 275 CE. Aurelian did much to arrest the decline that the empire had experienced in the previous forty years.

Aurelian had been a cavalry officer in the army of Gallienus, and his reign was marked by a number of important military successes. He successfully drove the **Vandals** from Pannonia and the Juthungi from the Danube region. Aurelian then had to defend northern Italy itself. A tribe called the **Alemanni** crossed the Po River, but Aurelian defeated them decisively. Because their attack had threatened Rome itself, Aurelian began the construction of a great protective wall around the city in 271 CE.

Aurelian pragmatically abandoned Dacia as being too difficult to defend. However, in the east, he was more aggressive. In 272 CE, he embarked on a campaign to recapture the lands lost to Queen Zenobia of Palmyra. He was immediately successful, as city after city surrendered to his forces. Aurelian then went on to Gaul, where he restored Roman rule in 274 CE.

On the domestic front, the economy was threatened with collapse, the result of Gallienus issuing virtually worthless coins. Aurelian called in much of the debased coinage and issued new coinage, reintroducing the *antoninianus*. This move did not altogether stem inflation, so to pacify the populace, he instituted a daily issue of bread, plus regular distributions of salt, oil, and pork.

Aurelian was outstandingly successful in restoring Roman authority throughout the empire, yet he, too, was eventually murdered by a group of officers. He was followed by a series of six competent generals over a nine-year period; all of them continued to purge the empire of invaders and revolutionaries.

The four members of Diocletian's tetrarchy are depicted in this fourth-century CE sculpture.

CHAPTER THREE

The End of the Empire

I n the third and fourth centuries CE, the Roman Empire was rarely united or stable. For much of the period, rival claimants fought each other for the throne. At the same time, the Germanic tribes of northern Europe constantly threatened the empire.

The third century CE saw the Roman Empire in crisis. Its economy was in ruins, its social order was disintegrating, and its army was too small to either police the enormous empire or protect its borders from foreign aggression.

The problems with the army were manifold. It was not only too small but also too static. Garrisons set up to protect the provinces or the frontiers rapidly became permanent towns, and many new recruits came from the local area. Far from Rome, the soldiers felt they owed allegiance only to their own legion and general, rather than to the emperor. Some units of the army consisted of tribal mercenaries, sometimes under their own chieftain. Such units were not amenable to traditional army discipline and resisted the rigorous training that characterized the army of old. Insubordination was rife, leading to frequent revolts and occasionally assassination of the commanders.

The army was also expensive to maintain. Military pay had been increased under Caracalla, and troop bonuses were often paid following a successful campaign. To augment the soldiers' pay, some generals allowed the legionnaires to plunder—even in the provinces. During the third century CE, the general population was victimized as frequently by Roman soldiers as by invading barbarians.

Disease and Economic Crises

As the empire grew ever more expensive to administer, successive emperors attempted to address the problem by debasing the coinage. They gradually decreased the proportion of gold, silver, and copper in the coins, which resulted in a decrease in their actual value. Prices soared, and rampant inflation brought poverty and misery to many of the citizens. In addition, the emperors levied the highest taxes in history.

The economic crisis hit trade hard. Artisans were unable to sell their products, and people had no money to buy imported goods. Increasingly, the provinces had to rely on their own resources. As the coinage became ever more worthless, barter became popular, and many taxes were paid in kind. This development made things difficult for tax collectors, who were personally responsible for delivering the correct amount of tax to the government. Many collectors tried to evade their commitment by disappearing into rural isolation.

Epidemics also contributed to the empire's general decline. Outbreaks of disease regularly wreaked havoc on the population, decimating it and reducing the supply of labor needed to work the land and repair roads and aqueducts. The number of slaves also declined because the army no longer engaged in profitable wars that brought tens of thousands of prisoners to the slave markets.

To make the most from their land, landowners turned to different ways of farming. Instead of using slaves to work an entire estate, owners leased parcels of land to farming families. These tenant farmers agreed to surrender a fixed share of all their income to the landowners. This arrangement, while it provided lower profits than before, did at least guarantee the landowners a regular income, which was important at a time when it was difficult to find a market for wine, oil, and other estate products.

The arrangement was also beneficial to the tenant farmers (or *coloni*, as they were called), providing some measure of protection in unsettled times. Occasionally, a small landowning farmer would even offer his acreage to a wealthy landowner in return for a contract as a tenant farmer. As the system became increasingly widespread, landowners attempted to tie their coloni to the land. In the fourth century CE, the emperors would force successive generations of coloni to stay on the estates, making them little better than serfs.

The Last of the Illyrian Emperors

After Emperor Aurelian died in 275 CE, the senate appointed an elderly senator called Tacitus to be his successor. Tacitus resigned (or was killed) in less than a year and was followed by the Illyrian general Probus. Probus successfully fought off a Gallic invasion and then turned his attention to economic reform. He employed the army on various public works programs, brought in barbarians to settle the provinces, and encouraged the cultivation of abandoned farms. These measures did not make him popular with the army, and he was assassinated by soldiers in 282 CE.

The army replaced Probus with Aurelius Carus, a general who shared power with his two sons, Numerian and Carinus. Carus and Numerian were both assassinated two years later while on campaign in Persia.

Diocletian, ruled 284–305 CE

After the death of Numerian in 284 CE, yet another Illyrian, called Diocles, seized power. The son of a farmer, he had risen through the ranks to become a popular general in the army of Carus. When Numerian was murdered by Aper (his father-in-law), Diocles promptly killed Aper and was himself proclaimed emperor by the troops. Changing his name to **Diocletian**, the new emperor subsequently defeated and killed Carinus.

Diocletian's hold on power was precarious. Persians threatened the empire in the east, while Germanic tribes harassed the north. The loyalty of Gaul was in question because of the *bacaudae* (armies of

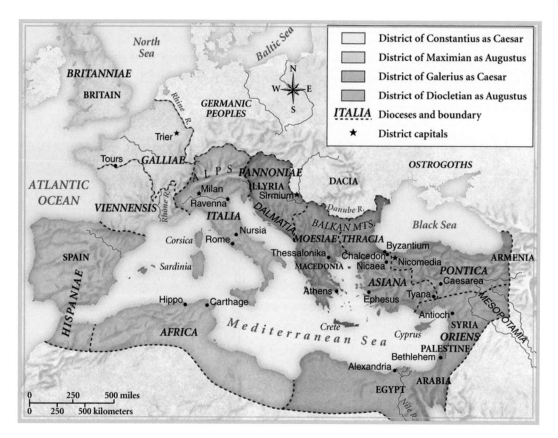

District of Constantius as Caesar

District of Maximian as Augustus

District of Galerius as Caesar

District of Diocletian as Augustus

ITALIA Dioceses and boundary

★ District capitals

escaped coloni reneging on their obligations) and displaced farmers ruined by war and exploitation. To reestablish Roman authority in these areas, Diocletian needed to send in experienced commanders. However, he was aware that, in the past, victorious generals had often seized power, as he himself had done. In order to bypass this problem, he decided to share power with his generals.

Establishing the Tetrarchy

Diocletian established a new form of government, a four-way sharing of imperial power called the tetrarchy. He first invited the general Maximian to share power, giving Maximian the titles Caesar (in 285 CE) and Augustus (in 286 CE). Then, in 293 CE, Diocletian selected two more generals and gave them each the title Caesar. He adopted one of them, **Galerius**, as his son, while Maximian adopted the other, Constantius. These generals were all Illyrians and were related to Diocletian either by marriage or adoption.

Each "emperor" was given a section of the empire to control, although no formal territorial division was made. Diocletian took the eastern part of the empire, consisting of Thrace, Egypt, and Asia, while Maximian had the Italian Peninsula and Africa. Galerius ruled the Danubian provinces, while the western provinces of Gaul, Spain, and Britain went to Constantius. Each emperor had his own capital city in his region; none of them resided in Rome. Diocletian retained overall supervision of the empire and the authority to legislate and appoint consuls.

The system effectively restored stability to the threatened areas and improved provincial government. Provincial armies were increased in size, particularly in the border areas, and landowners were required to contribute either money or recruits to the army. Diocletian also established a tactical army under his direct control. The tetrarchy effectively ended the supremacy of Rome and the Italian Peninsula and, by establishing separate centers of power in the eastern and western parts of the empire, paved the way for its eventual division.

On the domestic front, Diocletian instituted price controls on food and other necessities and established maximum wages for workers. These measures went some way toward curbing the raging inflation. He improved administrative efficiency in the provinces by appointing equites rather than senators as the administrators. These appointees were responsible for all aspects of civilian administration, including police and legal matters and, above all, taxation.

The changes that were implemented by Diocletian resulted in enormous increases in the costs of running the state, and these costs had to be met by the populace via increased taxes. To ensure that the taxes were paid, Diocletian organized the empire as a coercive state, enforcing universal cooperation in its maintenance. To preserve the status quo, he insisted that anyone practicing an important profession was compelled to continue it for life and that a son was to follow in his father's footsteps. The coloni, the tenant farmers who previously had some right to mobility, were henceforth tied to the land. These measures may have gone some way toward stabilizing society, but they came with a price. For many Roman citizens, freedom was now severely limited.

Diocletian was an autocrat, and he believed that he received his authority from the gods, with whom he would take his place after his death. However, Diocletian also wanted to be considered a god while he was still living, and he invoked Roman religious tradition to support the idea. Linking himself with Jupiter, Diocletian demanded to be known as Jovius and regarded as a holy person. This move put him in conflict with the Christians, who refused to take part in emperor worship. Incensed by the attitude of the Christians, and alarmed by the increasing number of them in the army and in his court, Diocletian became determined to put an end to Christianity once and for all.

The final, and fiercest, persecutions of Christians began in 303 CE, primarily in the east, where Diocletian himself reigned alongside Galerius. Diocletian ordered the destruction of churches and banned Christians from assembling to worship. Many Christians were killed, but regardless of how many martyrs died, the new faith was too firmly established to be extinguished. By the time Diocletian abdicated in 305 CE, the ferocity of the persecutions had diminished.

Constantine's Rise

After Diocletian had reigned for twenty years, he abdicated and forced Maximian to do the same. The two Caesars, Galerius and Constantius, became Augusti, and two new Caesars, Severus and Maximinus Daia, were appointed. Together, the four made up the second tetrarchy. In this way, Diocletian attempted to replace the hereditary principle with a system of appointing successors. Within a year, however, the system had broken down. When Constantius died in 306 CE at Eboracum (present-day York) in Britain, the armies of Gaul and Britain ignored the rules of the tetrarchy and proclaimed his son **Constantine** as Augustus. When he heard the news, Maximian's son Maxentius promptly had himself declared Augustus in Rome, ignoring both Galerius and Severus. Thus, in 307 CE, seven men were claiming to be Augustus (including another pretender in Africa). Civil war followed, but by 311 CE, several of the claimants had died by natural causes or been assassinated, leaving Constantine and Maxentius in the west and Licinius (who had been declared Augustus by Galerius) and Maximus Daia in the east.

Constantine, who was militarily the strongest among them, invaded Italy and defeated Maxentius near Rome in 312 CE. Maxentius drowned while trying to escape. During the campaign, Constantine claimed to have had a vision of the cross, and he later converted to Christianity. After his defeat of Maxentius, Constantine joined forces with Licinius. In 313 CE, they won over the Christians in the east by issuing the Edict of Milan, which guaranteed the Christians freedom of worship. Maximinus Daia was defeated by Licinius and died the same year.

Constantine emerged from the contest as the victor in the west, while Licinius ruled in the east. For a time, there was an uneasy truce between the two emperors, but in 324 CE, the tensions between them erupted into war. Licinius was forced to surrender, and he and his son were both executed.

The Rule of Constantine

Now the uncontested ruler of the Roman Empire, Constantine established a new administrative headquarters on the site of **Byzantium** and called it **Constantinople**. Situated on the Bosporus, a strait that links the Black Sea to the Mediterranean Sea, this small town occupied a strategic position between the Euphrates and Danube rivers and between the continents of Europe and Asia. It was therefore an important post on the overland trading routes between east and west, and it was destined to become a major city (present-day Istanbul).

Constantine, who had converted to Christianity sometime around 312 CE, now declared it to be the official religion of the Roman state. The traditional worship of the pagan gods was discouraged; their temples were ransacked and their treasure, together with that of Licinius, was used to benefit the state. To stabilize the currency, Constantine had a new gold coin minted, the *solidus*, which was to become the basic currency of the Byzantine Empire.

Constantine continued many of the reforms initiated by Diocletian, particularly that of separating civilian power from military power. He maintained the separate forces of border guards (*limitanei*) and tactical troops (*comitatenses*), and he expanded the authority of the Praetorian prefects, establishing four great prefectures: the east, the Italian Peninsula, Gaul, and Illyricum.

The Growth of Christianity

By the second century CE, Christianity was spreading throughout the eastern part of the Roman Empire, and Christian communities known as ecclesia (assemblies) were well established in Greece. Initially, the members of these communities were united only by their common faith, and there was no central authority either within the individual groups or over the church as a whole. In time, however, the administration of a community fell to one of its elders, who came to be called the *episcopus* (supervisor), the Greek word from which the word *bishop* is derived. A hierarchy of priests and lower clergy, variously termed *deacons* or *presbyters*, formed under the bishop.

By the third century CE, Christianity had spread to the west, and the bishop of Rome had particular influence. Rome was the city of the apostle Peter, the man Christ had said would be the rock on which he would build his church. Regarded as Peter's heir, each succeeding bishop of Rome was seen as the natural leader of the church and would be approached to arbitrate in any communal disputes.

However, the bishop of Rome had little overall authority. The church was actually a federation of separate communities operating on an individual basis. They cooperated to the extent of giving support in time of need, exchanging literature, and providing lodging for members of other communities. This very lack of a centralized structure appears to have been an advantage during times of persecution because the church could not be put out of action simply by seizing a few of its leaders.

The church grew steadily throughout the third century CE, and the Christians soon formed one of the largest religious groups in the empire. Solidarity, based on their faith, mutual support, and respect for their leaders, was their strength. Although they were often persecuted, they could escape death if they renounced their faith at the last moment. Perhaps many did so, but those who remained steadfast and died were honored as martyrs by the community, and it was believed that their souls went straight to heaven.

In the later part of the third century CE, the empire entered a period of prolonged crisis, when rival claimants fought for the imperial crown and inflation threatened to destroy the economy. Yet it was precisely in these disturbed times that the church gained even more converts. It seems that the promise of a better life in the hereafter and an eternal reward for the righteous appealed to many people.

This vault was used for Christian worship in the early fifth century CE. By that point, the Christian faith had spread throughout much of the Roman Empire.

Constantine's government was expensive. Among other measures, he organized a distribution of grain to the poor, which made him popular with that segment of the population but not with the taxpayers who had to fund the scheme. The burden fell most heavily on poor farmers and landholders, and resulted in widespread anger among taxpayers and corruption among tax collectors.

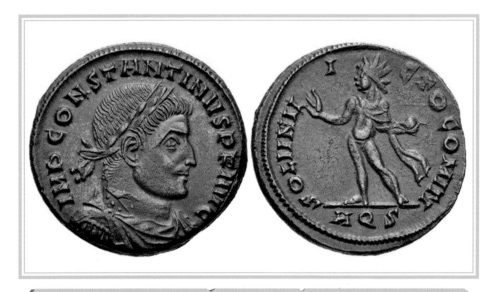

This gold coin depicts the emperor Constantine, who reunited the empire in 324 CE.

Constantine's death in 337 CE was followed by civil war, as his three sons battled for power. Eventually, in 353 CE, the only surviving son united the empire under his rule as Constantius II. During the eight years of his reign, the eastern border was under almost constant attack by the Persians, while on the Rhine and the Danube, marauding tribes made frequent raids. Constantius himself was only a mediocre general. However, his nephew Julian, whom he appointed Caesar and commander of the Roman army in Gaul, soon proved to be a brilliant military leader. Julian campaigned so successfully in Gaul that his troops declared him emperor in 361 CE. Civil war was averted when Constantius died in November of that year.

Julian and Jovian

Although he reigned for less than two years, Julian proved to be an extremely capable administrator. He took steps to curb the extravagance of his court, reduced the power of the secret police, and introduced a stable copper coinage. He renounced Christianity (earning himself the title **Julian the Apostate**) and reinstated the pagan religion, hoping to restore the traditional values of ancient Rome. Julian was killed fighting against the forces of the Persian Sassanid Empire in Mesopotamia in June of 363 CE.

Julian was replaced by Jovian, who was put in place by the army and lasted for only eight months. A moderate Christian, he attempted to restore religious tolerance to the empire. He succeeded in negotiating a peace with the Persian king Shapur II by ceding a considerable amount of territory, including the city of Nisibis and the whole of Armenia. Jovian died as the result of an accident in February of 364 CE. With his death, the empire was once again divided into east and west.

Valentinian and Valens

Valentinian I, a capable officer and another moderate Christian, was chosen by the army to be emperor in the west. The army insisted that he share power, so he appointed his less capable brother **Valens** as co-regent in the east. Valentinian proved to be an energetic defender of the empire. With the help of his general Theodosius the Elder, he fought a number of successful border campaigns in Gaul and Pannonia and put down insurrections in Britain and Africa. On the domestic front, he took steps to protect the poor, to maintain a strong administrative and tax collection system, and to encourage religious tolerance. Valentinian died suddenly in 375 CE in a freak manner; he burst a blood vessel in his brain while shouting at an ambassador from the Quadi tribe.

After the death of Valentinian, his sixteen-year-old son **Gratian** became emperor in the west, sharing his rule with his four-year-old brother Valentinian II. Gratian was a devout Christian and attempted to erase all traces of the ancient Roman religion from the empire.

In the east, Valens was less successful in defending his borders, which were continually raided by barbarian tribes, including the Visigoths from Dacia. The **Visigoths**, being harassed by the **Huns**, were driven south over the border and into Roman territory in 375 CE. Valens welcomed them, thinking that they could colonize depopulated land and supply recruits for his army. However, Roman officials began to mistreat the new arrivals, and in 376 CE, the Visigoths rebelled. Valens was forced to go to war.

The next two years saw a number of inconclusive battles. Finally, in 378 CE, Valens confronted an army of Gothic warriors outside Adrianople in Thrace. Earlier in the year, Gratian had driven back the Alemanni and the Goths from the border on the Danube. Valens had been advised to wait for the armies of his fellow emperor to join him before he confronted the Goths. He ignored the advice. In the ensuing battle, the Gothic cavalry inflicted a humbling defeat on the Roman forces. Valens himself died in combat. The Battle of Adrianople was a major turning point in the history of the Roman Empire; the Goths now had control of the Balkan Peninsula.

Gratian and Theodosius

After Valens's death, Gratian declared Theodosius emperor in the east in 379 CE. Theodosius was the son of Valentinian I's famous general Theodosius the Elder, who had been executed in a purge of Valentinian's supporters. Following in his father's footsteps, Theodosius was also an outstanding army general and was destined to emerge victorious from a very turbulent time. In 382 CE, he made peace with the Goths, giving them permission to live within the empire under their own laws and leaders. He did so only on condition that they served in his army.

In 383 CE, Magnus Maximus, the commander of the army in Gaul and Britain, was proclaimed emperor by his troops. He subdued Gaul and killed Gratian at Lyon. At first, Theodosius was disposed to recognize Maximus because they were both Spaniards and orthodox Christians. However, when Maximus invaded Italy, Theodosius met him in battle and killed him in 388 CE.

Valentinian II and Eugenius

Since 375 CE, Gratian had nominally shared the western throne with his brother Valentinian II. Theoretically, Valentinian ruled over Italy, Africa, and part of Illyricum, but because he was only four years old when he became emperor, power in the early years really rested with his mother, Justina. In 387 CE, when Maximus invaded Italy, Valentinian sought refuge with Theodosius, and after Maximus was killed, Theodosius reinstated Valentinian as the emperor of the west. However, Valentinian died in 392 CE, either by assassination or suicide. He was succeeded by Eugenius, who began to reestablish the worship of the old gods of Rome. This policy brought him into conflict with the Christian Theodosius.

Theodosius and Eugenius fought each other at the Battle of Frigidus River in 394 CE. Theodosius was victorious, making him emperor of both east and west. He was the last man to rule over a unified Roman Empire, but he died only four months later, in January of 395 CE. The empire was then divided between his two sons. The western empire was to collapse in the fifth century CE, while the eastern empire would survive for another thousand years.

Hagia Sophia was originally built as a church in the sixth century CE. After Constantinople fell to the Ottoman Turks in 1452 CE, the building was transformed into a mosque. Today, it serves as a museum operated by the Turkish government.

CHAPTER FOUR

The Rise of Constantinople

The city of Byzantium became the capital of the eastern Roman Empire in 324 CE and eventually acquired a new name: Constantinople. The city flourished commercially and became the center of the Christian world.

The city of Byzantium was founded by Greek colonists around the end of the eighth century BCE. It became famous for its favorable location; it lay on the Bosporus, a narrow strait that was part of a strategic waterway between the Black Sea and the Mediterranean Sea. The city thus occupied a crucial position between the continents of Asia and Europe. Byzantium had been granted the status of a free city by Rome in 65 BCE. However, over the following two centuries, it gradually lost most of its freedom. After the Byzantines supported the pretender Pescennius Niger against the Roman emperor Septimius Severus, Severus captured the city in 196 CE, razing the walls, massacring the citizens, and ending any remaining privileges.

Building Constantinople

Byzantium, by the early fourth century CE, was an impoverished city inhabited by downtrodden citizens. However, its fortunes were soon to change.

When the western Roman emperor Constantine defeated his eastern counterpart, Licinius, in 324 CE, he made Byzantium his new capital, renaming the city Constantinople. Once Constantine

The ancient walls of Constantinople can still be seen today.

decided to establish his new residence there, the city began to experience dizzying change and growth. Constantine commissioned ambitious architects to design him a city worthy of an emperor.

The city soon rang with the sound of masons' mallets cleaving blocks of stone as the grandiose plan rapidly took shape. In the city center, an army of workmen labored on the Mese, a wide boulevard destined to be the main shopping street. The road intersected with a splendid oval forum with opulent marble paving that covered the entire area. At the center of the forum, a marble plinth 20 feet (6 meters) high supported a pillar 100 feet (30 m) tall bearing a statue of Constantine. All around the forum, massive blocks of housing were erected, above which the domes of churches soon reached toward the sky. The emperor's palace stood on the eastern edge of the city, and sailors could see its bronze gates glittering in the sun from far away.

The new city became a magnet for members of the old senatorial families from Rome, who flocked to Constantinople in the hope of securing a grand house in the metropolis or a large country estate outside it. Poorer migrants also flooded in, lured by the promise of the free grain handouts that Constantine made available. To adorn his fabulous city, the emperor's fleets brought in treasures plundered from all over the empire.

On May 11, 330 CE, the city was officially dedicated as the new capital. It was commonly referred to as Nova Roma (New Rome), but the emperor called it Constantinople. The incoming stream of people from across the empire raised the population to several hundred thousand residents.

Constantine could not have established his headquarters at a place that was better situated. The city lay on a peninsula between the Sea of Marmara to the south and the **Golden Horn**, a narrow inlet of the Bosporus, to the north. This inlet extended more than 6 miles (9.6 kilometers) inland, providing ready access to the sea and its shipping routes. From the huge palaces on the shores of the Bosporus, the city stretched over seven hills to the massive wall that enclosed the peninsula to the west. This city rampart ran from the Golden Horn in the north to the Sea of Marmara in the south and was located some 2.5 miles (4 km) west of the ancient city.

As Byzantium continued to grow during the fourth century CE, it started to extend beyond this wall, and in the early fifth century CE, the emperor Theodosius II constructed another wall, farther west, which also enclosed the entire peninsula. This second wall made the city virtually impregnable. In fact, Constantinople was only taken by force twice in its history—by the Crusaders in 1204 CE and by the Ottoman Turks in 1453 CE. Large sections of its impressive fortifications can still be seen today.

Urban Development

Busy trade routes led east to Anatolia and west to Italy and Spain. Constantinople's spacious harbors were filled with commercial ships carrying goods to distant destinations. Its location, prosperity, and official protection made the city the crucial interface between east and west. It became known as the emporium, the commercial center of the world.

Constantine intended the city to be a second Rome, and it was given an administration modeled on that of the old capital, complete with a senate. However, Constantinople differed from Rome in several important aspects. Whereas Rome was a Latin city, Constantinople was Greek in both language and culture. It was also a Christian city from its very beginnings. There were no pagan temples in Constantine's capital, only Christian churches.

Unlike Rome, which had developed in an ad hoc way, Constantinople was meticulously planned. The design of the new capital was intended to avoid the crisscrossing nightmare of alleys, *insulae* (public apartment houses), markets, arches, and temples that typified Rome. Instead, Constantinople was to be a reflection of imperial might, and its well-organized street plan featured large squares, broad avenues, and carefully calculated building lines.

However, behind the main streets, private builders went their own way, particularly after Constantine's death. The result, despite the overall plan, was chaos. Before long, a tangle of small streets and alleyways covered the hills. The houses and shops in these streets were shoddily constructed of wood, clay, and straw and were unable to withstand the earthquakes that frequently affected the city. The earthquakes were invariably followed by fires, which spread rapidly from house to house, destroying entire neighborhoods. The methods for fighting these fires were completely inadequate; small buckets of water and primitive hand pumps were no match for the conflagrations. However, the Valens Aqueduct, completed in 368 CE (see sidebar, page 49), at least improved the water supply.

Constantinople was divided into fourteen districts, each with its own administration. Local officials were responsible for public services and for public order. As each neighborhood developed its own characteristics, residents tended to be categorized by neighborhood. Every Byzantine citizen aspired to own a villa in District IV, which was the royal quarter. The area was home to the wealthy and powerful, who lived clustered around the impressive complex of the court. As the royal palace grew, it became, over time, a small city in itself, with the villas of court dignitaries adjoining the harbor basin. The palaces were surrounded by beautiful gardens. The buildings were connected by marble arcades, where ministers, ladies of the court, eunuchs, and power-hungry church officials congregated and schemed for favor from the emperor.

Exploring the City

Constantine had attracted adventurers from all over the empire to his new city. Most of the populace came from the eastern part of

Valens's Aqueduct

Valens's aqueduct was built in the late fourth century CE. Today, modern city streets weave between the aqueduct's arches.

The emperor Valens, who ruled from 364 to 378 CE, built an impressive aqueduct to bring water to the city, using stones taken from Chalcedon, an ancient Greek seaport on the opposite side of the Bosporus from Constantinople. The aqueduct fed tremendous reservoirs in cisterns carved out of the rock beneath the city. Some of these reservoirs were entirely underground, but their supporting pillars, which would never be seen except by torchlight, were lavishly decorated. The water was fed to fountains and bathhouses in the city, and the reservoirs guaranteed a supply of water even if the aqueduct were to be destroyed.

This fifteenth-century CE illuminated manuscript shows the walled city of Constantinople. The city's strategic location and impressive defenses made it difficult to attack.

the empire, with Greek and Syrian elements predominating, giving Constantinople the atmosphere of a frontier city.

At the city center was the square called the Augustaion, named after Constantine's mother, Augusta Helena. Other important landmarks in the center were the bronze gates to the palaces, the **Hagia Sophia** (the Church of Holy Wisdom), the senate, and the enormous Hippodrome (where horse races were held). The Mese was the most important street in the entire empire. It was lined with arcades on both sides to protect strollers from the sun. Goods from all corners of the world were displayed there, and every craft was practiced under its porticos. At night, however, the Mese showed another face of the metropolis; the arcades became the domain of sleeping beggars. The city's grandeur concealed the fact that much of the population lived in poverty, often kept alive only by the free grain distributed by the emperor.

This grain handout was given to every registered father of a family. The government also made attempts to control the prices of other foodstuffs to prevent the poor from starving. On the whole, there were adequate supplies of food in the city, but there were occasional catastrophic instances of famine. These food shortages were dangerous because two hundred thousand hungry people posed an enormous threat to the stability of the government.

Sport in Constantinople

One aspect of life that was imported from Rome was horse racing. The sport took place in the Hippodrome, which could accommodate more than fifty thousand spectators. Here, the common people could watch not only sporting events, but other great civic occasions, such as military triumphs.

This illustration imagines what the Constantinople hippodrome might have looked like.

The emperor and his cortege, who were usually among the spectators, sat above the stalls in the Kathisma (the royal box), which was directly connected to the royal palace. For the ordinary man, the presence of the Kathisma offered an opportunity for him to express his political opinions. In the anonymity of the Hippodrome, an individual could freely air his view of the emperor by cheering either for the emperor's horses or for a rival chariot.

The organization of the games that took place in the Hippodrome lay in the hands of two clubs, the **Greens** and the **Blues**. Over the years, these clubs developed into powerful syndicates that managed every aspect of entertainment in the Hippodrome. Every charioteer, trainer, groom, and stable hand belonged to one club or the other. The jockeys appeared on the track clad in either green or blue colors, and most Byzantine citizens supported a specific club. The odds in the Hippodrome were a major topic of conversation in the city, and the competition between the clubs was extremely fierce; the races often ended in bloody riots.

The two clubs also acquired administrative and political importance. In an emergency, they could mobilize the population to guard the city walls. The members of the two clubs tended to be drawn from different social classes and to have different religious and political preferences. The Blues were orthodox Christians, oriented toward a rural and traditional lifestyle, while the Greens found their supporters among the merchants and lower classes. Being a supporter of one club or the other was often an emotional matter, however. It was also not always clear what each of the parties represented or was aiming at, apart from triumphing over the other.

The emperor needed to be attuned to the sensitivities of both the Greens and the Blues. The court was generally sympathetic to the Blues, although an astute ruler would keep both parties busy so that they did not have time to turn against him. On the days of the most important races (Christmas Day and May 11, the anniversary of the founding of the city), the streets were deserted, and cries of *mika* (conquer!) resounded from the Hippodrome. Troops waited behind the great arena ready to subdue any possible riot. If things failed to go their way, even the emperor's supporters might suddenly turn into revolutionaries.

Popular Rule

The emperor's authority was based, to some extent, upon the agreement of the people. An orderly system of succession existed only in theory. Some emperors came to power after public riots in their favor. Others gained the crown after a palace revolution, or through a conspiracy, or because they were the choice of the widow of the deceased ruler. Some emperors trained a favorite to be the successor, while other emperors left the matter to their survivors. After a new emperor gained palace favor, he would have himself acclaimed emperor in the Hippodrome. Only then would he be given the outward trappings of power from the patriarch (head of the church). This act gave the populace a visible sign of the succession.

In the popular view, the emperor was God's chosen one. However, this belief did not prevent dissidents from attempting to overthrow the emperor. The thinking was that, if such an attempt were successful, it would be proof that God had switched his support to the usurper. Consequently, the position of the emperor was always precarious, making Constantinople a troubled and dangerous city.

Theological Controversies

In the early days of Constantinople, the Christian world was riven by bitter ideological disputes. The most important involved the doctrine of **Arianism**, which was formulated by the Alexandrian priest Arius (ca. 250–336 CE). The doctrine stated that Jesus Christ was a created being and not of the same substance as God. This belief ran contrary to the orthodox view that God, Christ, and the Holy Spirit were three aspects of one divine being. The Arian view was considered heresy by the orthodox church, and was condemned in 325 CE at the First Ecumenical Council, held at **Nicaea**. However, Constantine I reinstated banished Arian bishops in 334 CE, and it was also supported by his son and successor, Constantius II. Valens, who became emperor in 364 CE, was also an Arian. However, when Theodosius came to the throne in 379 CE, he outlawed Arianism in favor of orthodox Christianity.

In the fifth century CE, another religious controversy split the church. Again the central issue was the nature of Christ. This time, the cause of the problem was the advent of the doctrine of **Monophysitism**, a term derived from the Greek words *monos* (single) and *physis* (nature). According to this doctrine, Christ had only a single nature, which was divine, not human. This position conflicted with the orthodox view that Christ was both divine and human. In 451 CE, Pope Leo I convened the Fourth Ecumenical Council in Chalcedon to resolve the controversy. However, the ensuing edict of the council failed to reconcile the opposing views. In the east, the debate continued to rage. The people of Syria and Egypt generally opted for the Monophysitic concept, but in Constantinople, there was no consensus. The Monophysites found many advocates among the lower classes of Constantinople, but they also had supporters among the highest ranks. One such supporter in the highest ranks was Emperor **Anastasius I**.

Anastasius, who came to the throne in 491 CE after the death of Emperor Zeno (see sidebar, page 55), was a competent administrator. He developed a strong, well-disciplined army that he used to good effect in battles against the rebelling Isaurians, the Persians, and the invading Slavs and Huns. However, Anastasius did not endear himself to the citizens of Constantinople when he tried to put an end to the widely enjoyed fights between gladiators and animals or when he attempted to abolish some popular dances that he considered to be immoral. When Anastasius openly supported the Monophysitic cause, his popularity plummeted.

Although he was a layman, Anastasius had voiced his beliefs in scholarly sermons before taking the throne. Throughout his reign, he supported the Monophysites on every possible occasion, causing great offense to the Blue party, which was more orthodox in its religious views. On Sunday, November 4, 512 CE, the priest in the Hagia Sophia offered up a Monophysitic prayer during mass. The Blues were shocked and affronted. After the service, they called for a new emperor, and fights broke out with the Greens. Violent uprisings followed, and within a few days, the entire city was in an uproar. Rioters even set fire to the houses of the emperor's family.

Anastasius decided to confront his people. Dressed in simple clothes, and without his crown, he appeared in the royal box in the Hippodrome, where twenty thousand rebels booed him. When the crowd had quieted down, the emperor humbly asked for forgiveness and even offered to resign. The rebels were dumbfounded. Then, some of the emperor's supporters, who had been placed among the crowd, shouted, "Long live Anastasius!" The cry was taken up by others, and what might have been Anastasius's downfall became a triumph. Anastasius promised the people he would make some religious concessions and then withdrew to the palace while the rebels went quietly home.

That same day, Anastasius began making a series of arrests. Having subdued the revolutionaries, he started on a course of reprisals. The instigators of the insurgency paid with their lives, and the emperor pursued his former policies with more determination than ever.

The insurrection against Anastasius followed a pattern that was only too frequent in Constantinople. Religious dissent would lead to an outburst; the emperor would silence the masses with empty promises; and then he would take his revenge. Although rebellions occurred frequently in Constantinople, they were usually too spontaneous to be successful.

Zeno's Reign

The eastern emperor Zeno, who ruled from 474 to 491 CE, was born in Isauria, a region in central Anatolia. The Isaurians, who had the reputation of being aggressive savages, had originally been conquered by the Romans in the first century BCE. In the reign of Augustus, Isauria was annexed and became part of the Roman province of Galatia. Zeno became commander of an Isaurian army in the service of the eastern emperor Leo I. Zeno came into such favor that he married the emperor's daughter, Ariadne, in 466 CE. When Leo died in 474 CE, he was succeeded by his grandson (Zeno's son). When the child also died before the year was out, Zeno himself became emperor.

Zeno's reign was a troubled one. His Isaurian advisor, Illus, proved to be a turncoat more than once. Illus first engineered a coup, putting Basiliscus (the late emperor's brother-in-law) on the throne and forcing Zeno to flee for safety to Isauria. Then, changing sides, Illus helped Zeno regain the throne in 476 CE. Eight years later, Illus headed a rebellion in Anatolia. He was finally defeated and executed in 488 CE.

Zeno also had to contend with uprisings among the **Ostrogoths** and bitter dissension within the church between Monophysitism and orthodoxy.

In 482 CE, he wrote a letter, called the Henotikon, in which he attempted to bring about a reconciliation between the opposing factions. Zeno died in 491 CE. Legend has it that he was buried alive by mistake.

This mosaic of Jesus Christ is from the Hagia Sophia. Christianity became the dominant religion during the reign of Emperor Constantine.

CHAPTER FIVE

Christianity's Ascendance

One of the most important developments to occur in the Roman Empire in the third century CE was the abandonment of the old gods of Rome and the adoption of Christianity as the official state religion.

Christians living in the Roman Empire had been persecuted since the reign of Nero in the first century CE. Some persecutions, particularly that of Diocletian, had been especially virulent. Christians had often been forced to give up their faith publicly, or be crucified or thrown to the animals in the arena. However, in the early fourth century CE, the situation changed when a new emperor embraced the faith himself and made it the state religion.

Constantine's Conversion

When Constantine was proclaimed emperor by his troops in Britain in 306 CE, he had to fight to retain his throne. Among several rivals was Maxentius (the son of the former emperor Maximian), who declared himself emperor in Rome. In 312 CE, while on campaign in Italy to meet up with Maxentius, Constantine dreamed that Christ told him to have the monogram XP (the first two Greek letters of the name of Christ) inscribed on the shields of his soldiers. Constantine followed these instructions, and the following day (the very day he was to meet Maxentius in battle), he had a vision in which he saw the same sign and the Latin words *in hoc signo vinces* (in this sign you will conquer)

Before his victory at Milvian Bridge, Constantine experienced a divine vision. Constantine was led to order his troops to paint the Christian Chi-Rho on their shields.

superimposed on the sun. When he defeated Maxentius at the **Battle of Milvian Bridge** on that day, Constantine attributed his victory to the influence of Jesus Christ.

Won over to the cause of Christianity, Constantine ended the persecution of the Christians when he finally became emperor. In 313 CE, he and his co-emperor Licinius issued the Edict of Milan. This proclamation guaranteed Christians freedom of worship and returned property confiscated by the state during the times of persecution.

Freed from constraints, the Christian church now attracted many converts. Bishops everywhere could count on the emperor's support, which became evident when Constantine assumed sole rule of the Roman Empire in 324 CE. He gave vast landholdings to the Christian communities, especially to that based in Rome, and within a few years, the church had become one of the largest landowners in the empire.

The bishop of Rome rapidly gained moral and ecclesiastical authority over all the other Christian communities, and the foundation for a hierarchical church was laid as the emperor moved toward making Christianity the state religion.

Consolidating Doctrine

In 325 CE, Constantine convoked the first empire-wide meeting of church dignitaries in an effort to resolve a dispute about the mystery of the Trinity. At issue was Arius's doctrine of Arianism (see sidebar, page 60), which maintained that the Son of God could not have the same nature as God himself. Determined that his new church should not be weakened by internal feuding, Constantine convened a council at the city of Nicaea in Anatolia. The meeting was attended by 318 bishops. Some of the bishops agreed with Arius, while others vehemently condemned him. The bishops of Nazianzus and Antioch both spoke powerfully against Arianism, while **Athanasius** of Alexandria maintained (in defense of orthodoxy) that Christ had two natures—human and divine.

This sixteenth-century CE painting depicts the Council of Nicaea, which condemned the doctrine of Arianism.

Understanding Arianism

In the fourth century CE, the church was divided by the doctrine of Arianism, which concerned the nature of Jesus Christ and originated with the teachings of an Alexandrian priest called Arius (ca. 250–336 CE). Arius maintained that Christ was not one with and indivisible from God the Father but had, in fact, been created by the Father at some point in time and therefore was not fully divine.

The doctrine of Arianism flew right in the face of the church's doctrine of the Trinity, which affirmed that God the Father, God the Son, and God the Holy Spirit were all of the same substance and constituted one God. This doctrine of the Trinity was reaffirmed by the Council of Nicaea in 325 CE when it issued a creed stating that the Son is of one substance (*homoousios*) with the Father.

Although Arianism was outlawed by the Council of Nicaea, it was not extinguished. It continued to surface throughout the following decades and was even officially recognized during the reigns of Constantius II and Valens. The doctrine also gave rise to a lesser heresy called Semi-Arianism. Whereas the true Arians maintained that the Son was of a different substance from the Father, the Semi-Arians held that Christ was of like substance (*homoiousios*) to him. The fact that only the letter *i* (iota in Greek) differentiated the orthodox doctrine from that of the Semi-Arians may have given rise to the expression, "There's not an iota of difference between them."

Eventually, the council issued the **Nicene Creed**, which affirmed that Christ was consubstantial with God and described Christ as "God from God, Light from Light, true God from true God, begotten not created, of one being with the Father." The controversial teachings of Arius were banned as heresy. Constantine exiled the priest and his major supporters and declared the Nicene Creed to be state law.

Constantine's attitude toward the Nicene Creed was ambivalent. He was not himself much concerned by matters of doctrine, and he was reluctant to antagonize the large group of Arian supporters who were influential in his court. Eusebius, the bishop of Caesarea in Palestine, leaned toward Arianism, and he managed to persuade Constantine to recall Arius from exile in 334 CE and to banish Athanasius instead.

Competing Interpretations

The battle between Arianism and orthodoxy continued after Constantine's death in 337 CE. His son, Constantius II, supported the Arian doctrine, as did the influential bishop Eusebius of Nicomedia, who was made bishop of Constantinople in 339 CE. By 359 CE, Arianism had been made the state religion, but two factions had evolved. Extreme proponents of Arianism maintained that Christ was "unlike" God the Father, while moderate adherents (the Semi-Arians) declared that Christ was "of similar substance" to him.

When Valens became emperor in 364 CE, he persecuted the Semi-Arians. However, in 379 CE, orthodoxy triumphed once more when the emperor Theodosius came to the throne. He held the Second Ecumenical Council in Constantinople in 381 CE. This meeting reaffirmed the Nicene Creed and outlawed Arianism. From that time onward, the only people who still adhered to Arius's teachings were some Germanic tribes on the fringes of the empire. Those tribes had been converted to Christianity by Arian priests and were to hold their Arian beliefs until the seventh century CE.

The Church Grows

The emperor Constantine, who had done so much for Christianity, was finally baptized on his deathbed. All of his successors, apart from the emperor Julian, were Christians, and in this benign environment, Christianity grew and flourished. However, as the Christian communities grew, the church became more formalized. Small gatherings of believers, held perhaps in a private house, gave way to large ceremonial meetings in a church, and the meal of communion became the formalized ritual of mass.

The bishops became notable figures in the empire. They were given jurisdiction over a geographical territory, rather than their flock of the faithful. Because the bishops' temporal authority made the church easier to control, the emperors endorsed this hierarchy.

This thirteenth-century CE fresco depicts the Donation of Constantine, in which the emperor allegedly transferred authority over Rome and the rest of the Western Empire to the Pope. It is widely accepted that the event never actually happened, however.

In the east, the bishops of Jerusalem, Antioch, and Alexandria became known as patriarchs, and each of these cities developed as an autonomous center of Christianity. Constantinople, made the capital of the empire under Constantine, developed rapidly in the fourth century CE, and Theodosius, emperor of the east, bestowed the title of patriarch on its bishop in 381 CE. His authority now rivaled that of the bishop of Rome.

In the west, the bishop of Rome reigned supreme in the church. He was the only western patriarch, and he was called *Pappas* (Papa). This Greek form of address became Pope, the official title for the head of the Roman Catholic Church. In the fifth century CE, the pope would claim church supremacy over the state and acquire actual political power over the western Roman Empire.

Holding onto Paganism

Adherents to the traditional Roman religion of pagan gods had been left to worship as they pleased under Constantine, but his son Constans I, as emperor in the west, outlawed the worship of Greco-Roman gods within city limits. However, he stipulated that temples outside the cities should be respected. He probably did not want to alienate the rural population, most of whom remained true to the old religion.

Paganism was not easily eradicated, even in the cities. Smoke still rose from offerings to the Olympian gods, as it had for centuries, and many people still adhered to the cult of the **Eleusinian Mysteries**. In the Academy that Plato had founded in Athens, philosophers now debated the merits of Plato's ideals versus the new faith of Christianity.

Debating the Nature of God

During the debate about Arianism, another controversy arose concerning the Trinity. A group called the Pneumatomachi (warriors against the spirit) insisted that the Holy Spirit was also created, like the Son. This denied the concept of the Trinity—the doctrine that maintains that God exists as three persons (the Father, the Son, and the Holy Spirit) united as one. This doctrine is not explicit in the New Testament, however. There, the word *God* usually refers to the Father. The phrase *Spirit of God*, which is used throughout the New Testament, usually refers to the presence of God.

Although this confusion about the nature of the Holy Spirit was part of the Arian controversy, it was not fully addressed at the Council of Nicaea. It was not until the early fifth century CE, with the work of the theologian **Augustine**, that the concept of the Holy Trinity became firmly established as part of Christian doctrine.

Constans's brother, Constantius II, became sole ruler of the entire empire in 353 CE. A strong advocate of Arian Christianity, he was intolerant of paganism. He ordered a summary death penalty for anyone making sacrificial offerings at night, although public offerings in daylight were still allowed. In 361 CE, the situation was reversed when his cousin Julian came to the throne. Although reared as a Christian, Julian equated the rampant corruption and intrigue in the empire with the Christianity of Constantine. Julian took forceful measures to reform the administration and to restore worship of

Flavius Claudius Julianus (Julian the Apostate), ruled 355–363 CE

the Greco-Roman gods. Dubbed the Apostate for his beliefs, he discriminated against Christians and supported pagan cults. He forbade Christians to teach in schools and wrote vehement pamphlets against Christianity, siding with theological rebels within the church in order to foment discord. He organized a mystical anti-church and, in his palace, made animal sacrifices to the sun at dawn and dusk.

After a short reign, Julian died on campaign in Mesopotamia in 363 CE and was replaced by Jovian, the Christian commander of the palace guard. During his eight-month reign, Jovian restored the moderate policies of Constantine. While the Christians enjoyed his favor, he left the pagans to worship as they pleased. This policy continued under the emperor Valentinian I, who also tolerated the old religion while adhering to Christianity.

After Valentinian's death in 375 CE, his sons, Gratian and Valentinian II, became co-rulers. Throughout his reign, Gratian tried to eliminate all traces of paganism from the empire, beginning by refusing to take the traditional imperial title of *pontifex maximus* (chief priest). He abolished state financial support for pagan cults and, more controversially, ordered the ancient statue of Victory to be removed from the senate.

The Senate's Appeal

The senate was the last bastion of Roman traditionalism. Most of the senators came from families loyal to the Greco-Roman gods and tried to maintain the traditions of Rome during sessions of the senate. However, after the imperial court had been relocated to

Christians and the Law

For the first three centuries CE, Christians were widely persecuted; in many cases, they were forced to worship in secret. However, the situation changed in 313 CE, when Constantine issued the Edict of Milan, which granted legal rights to Christians and promised religious tolerance for all. This edict ushered in an era when Christianity, no longer operating under the threat of persecution, spread rapidly throughout the Roman Empire. Imperial legislation under Constantine favored the Christian church. He and later emperors established a series of laws that reinforced Christian ideals and values.

Constantine issued legislation relating to marriage as early as 313 CE, when it was decreed that adultery by either a husband or wife would be punishable by death. The method of execution was extremely unusual. The guilty party was to be tied up in a sack along with a snake and a dog and thrown into the sea. It is not known how often this sentence was actually carried out.

In 326 CE, the rape of a virgin was declared a crime punishable by death, a measure that may have been intended to protect the growing number of celibate Christian women. Divorce was permitted in a number of limited cases in 331 CE.

While Christian ideals were supported by these measures, other edicts sought to suppress the pagan religion and its traditions.

One set of measures was aimed particularly at heathen practices. People performing magic rituals were threatened with the death penalty in 318 CE. A year later, this penalty was extended to those involved in private sacrifices made for the purpose of divining the will of the gods by studying the entrails of the sacrificed animal. All sacrifices were forbidden in 341 CE, but the law was generally interpreted to mean only nocturnal and private sacrifices. Nocturnal sacrifices were barred again in 353 CE, and all pagan temples were ordered to be closed in 356 CE (an order that was widely disregarded). In 381 CE, all animal sacrifices to the gods were banned yet again, and in 392 CE, all pagan cults were outlawed.

Constantinople, the senate in Rome lost most of its influence, being relegated to the status of a town council. The desperate senators sent emissaries to Gratian, imploring him to return the statue of Victory to its proper place, but the emperor did not even deign to receive the delegation. Later, under the emperor Valentinian II, the senators tried again for an audience. This time, they succeeded, and Valentinian agreed to listen to their arguments. The consul Symmachus delivered a speech on their behalf.

Symmachus was a noted orator and writer who had tried to revive the culture of Rome's Golden Age. His plea to Valentinian was a classic example of rhetoric. "Allow me to confess the religion of my fathers," he began, "and do not harbor a grudge against it. This religion subjected the universe to its laws. It helped our ancestors to drive off Hannibal and to defend the Capitol against the barbarians." After saying that there should be no reason to reject the religion that made Rome great, Symmachus continued, "The god to whom we address our pleas is the same to all. The same heaven arches above our heads and we see the same stars and we are part of the same universe. The manner how one addresses one's maker is of little importance." After defending his religion, Symmachus went on to describe how priests and priestesses had been robbed of their income by various improprieties. The oration, later published and widely distributed, created a great stir in intellectual circles.

Ambrose, bishop of Milan, rebutted the arguments of Symmachus. "Everyone must serve the emperor," he began, addressing the emperor himself, "but the emperor must be humble before God. If you rule against God in this matter, the bishops will abandon you; you will enter the churches and not find a single priest to receive you." Then, speaking directly to Symmachus, he swept away his arguments with irony. "You say that the gods saved Rome from Hannibal. Why were the gods so slow to react during the Punic Wars? Had they decided to save Rome before the Battle of Cannae [a disastrous defeat in which thirty thousand Roman soldiers were killed] how many lives could have been spared?" Ambrose's words confirmed Valentinian in his views. He refused to restore the statue of Victory to the senate, and his successor, in spite of two more delegations, likewise refused.

Forcing Christianity on the Empire

Theodosius became emperor in the east in 379 CE. He was an extreme advocate of orthodox Christianity and showed no tolerance toward paganism whatsoever. He issued orders to destroy the altars and sanctuaries of the traditional gods throughout his empire, and he appointed special commissioners to see to the closing of the temples and the destruction of cult objects. These measures against paganism were profoundly unpopular and led to violent riots and lynchings. In one particularly insensitive incident, the bishop of Tours led a group of monks around Gaul felling the sacred oaks of the Celts.

A more sensational event took place in Alexandria at the Serapeum, an enormous temple that had been the place of worship of the Egyptian god Serapis ever since Ptolemy I had established the cult early in the third century BCE. After Theodosius ordered the temple to be closed, the followers of Serapis locked themselves in the building and defended it as best they could. Discouraged by the size of the mob that stormed the temple, they finally surrendered, after which a number of Christians entered the holy chamber and began to hack everything to pieces.

In the center of the chamber stood a huge wooden statue of Serapis, which was covered with bronze plates. When a soldier climbed up the statue and struck it in the face with an ax, one of the bronze plates fell to the ground. Other zealous Christians fell on the colossus, stripped it of its bronze covering, and set fire to the remains.

It was Theodosius's aim to make Christianity the only religion practiced in his realm, and he stated that it was his wish that none of his subjects would dare to worship idols. He demanded that every citizen of the empire adopt the religion that (in the words of the Council of Nicaea) "the apostle Peter had taught the Romans and that the Pontiff Damasus and Bishop Peter of Alexandria are currently teaching."

Theodosius's Mistake

In 390 CE, Theodosius was responsible for an atrocity in Greece. A group of people in Thessalonica was charged with rebelling against the emperor, and in retribution, he had seven thousand people massacred,

Bishop Ambrose of Milan famously excommunicated Emperor Theodosius I for orchestrating a massacre in Thessalonica, Greece.

although many of them were completely innocent. The pope condemned the massacre, and Bishop Ambrose of Milan excommunicated Theodosius, demanding that he do public penance. The emperor was forced to dress in a hair shirt and beg forgiveness from the bishop before the altar of Milan Cathedral, while the congregation looked on approvingly. The bishop then ordered Theodosius to do penance for another eight months before he would be readmitted to the church.

From the point of view of non-Christians, Theodosius had made a fool of himself. He had bowed to the will of a few people, rather than that of an almighty deity. Theodosius could not allow such a view to prevail, and he and his officials continued their persecution with renewed vigor, attacking both pagans and Christian dissidents alike.

After the death of Theodosius in 395 CE, the oppression that he had made official state policy rapidly disappeared in Constantinople. Elsewhere, however, pagans were still persecuted and discriminated against. In 415 CE, the noted female philosopher Hypatia, the last in a long line of sages who had brought distinction to the school of Alexandria, was slain in the street by a gang of fanatical monks. In Athens, however, despite the oppression, Plato's Academy continued to flourish. Throughout the fifth century CE, philosophers taught Platonism tempered by mysticism. However, the school was forced to close on the orders of the emperor **Justinian I** in 529 CE.

As Roman power waned, Rome faced increased pressure from barbarian invasions, leading to several violent sacks of the city.

CHAPTER SIX

The Barbarian Invasions

In the late fifth century CE, the western Roman Empire finally collapsed under the onslaught of the various peoples who lived beyond its boundaries. The so-called barbarians formed new kingdoms that would shape the future of Europe.

As the Roman Empire started to crumble during the fourth and fifth centuries CE, it was subjected to repeated attacks and invasions by peoples that lived outside its boundaries. The Romans called these people *barbarians*, but the word did not have the negative connotations it has today. For the Romans, it simply meant "foreigner"—someone who was not a Roman. Goths, Huns, Vandals, and Franks crossed the frontiers and settled in the western empire. The deposition of the last western emperor in 476 CE marked the end of the empire.

The Goths

Some of the earliest peoples to occupy Roman territory were Goths. Historians are not sure where the Goths originated. In the sixth century CE, the Gothic historian Jordanes reported the legend that they had come from Scandinavia and sailed in three ships across the Baltic Sea to settle in what is now Germany.

Goths lived in Germany by the second century BCE, when two Gothic tribes invaded Gaul. By the fourth century CE, the Goths controlled a vast region from the Baltic to the Black Sea. Around 370 CE, Gothic tribes divided their territory. The Ostrogoths (from the

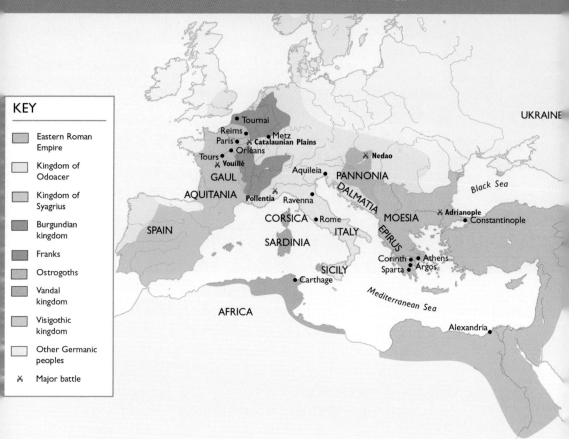

KEY

- Eastern Roman Empire
- Kingdom of Odoacer
- Kingdom of Syagrius
- Burgundian kingdom
- Franks
- Ostrogoths
- Vandal kingdom
- Visigothic kingdom
- Other Germanic peoples
- ✗ Major battle

UKRAINE

Tournai
Reims
Paris ✗ Catalaunian Plains
Metz
Orléans
Tours ✗ Vouillé
✗ Nedao
GAUL
Aquileia
PANNONIA
AQUITANIA Pollentia Ravenna
Black Sea
SPAIN
CORSICA •Rome
MOESIA
DALMATIA
✗ Adrianople
Constantinople
ITALY
EPIRUS
SARDINIA
Corinth •Athens
Sparta • Argos
SICILY
Carthage
Mediterranean Sea
AFRICA
Alexandria

Latin term for "eastern Goths") took the territory east of the Dniester River along the Black Sea, while the Visigoths (from the Latin term for "noble Goths") took the territory to the west, between the Dniester and the Danube.

The Visigoths

The Visigoths constantly raided the Danube border of the eastern Roman Empire. When they in turn were threatened by the advance of the Huns, a fierce people from the east, the Visigoths fled by crossing the frontier in 375 CE. The eastern Roman emperor Valens allowed the Visigoths to settle in the Roman province of Moesia, south of the Danube, on condition that they defend the border.

The arrangement soon turned sour. The Visigoths flouted the peace by looting, and Valens eventually felt obliged to stop them. The Visigoths proved an effective fighting force, however. They defeated

Valens at Adrianople in Thrace in 378 CE; the emperor died in the battle (see sidebar, page 75).

The emperor **Theodosius I** succeeded Valens and made peace with the Visigoths, letting them remain within the empire. They were allowed to retain their own laws and leaders as long as their troops served in the Roman army as mercenaries. Under Theodosius, the Roman Empire was for a brief time—and for the last time— united. On his death in 395 CE, the empire was divided between his sons, **Honorius** (age twelve), who took the west, and Arcadius (age eighteen) who took the east. Soon after Theodosius's death, the Visigoths elected a new, dynamic king, **Alaric I**.

The Rise of Alaric I

Alaric (ca. 370–410 CE) was born into a noble Gothic family and served for a time in the Roman army, commanding Gothic troops. After the death of Theodosius, Alaric left the army and was elected king of the Visigoths. With the military skills he had learned as a Roman commander, the twenty-five-year-old Alaric assembled a Visigothic army and embarked on a march south in search of new lands to settle. Accompanied by women and children, this massive migration of Gothic peoples occupied Illyricum and plundered Greece, sacking Corinth, Argos, and Sparta. Alaric was eventually halted and defeated by a Roman army and forced back to Epirus. There, he concluded a peace agreement in 397 CE with the eastern emperor Arcadius, under which Alaric was made prefect of the province of Illyricum, where he settled with his people.

By 401 CE, Alaric was on the move again. The Visigoths marched toward Italy and arrived on the Po Plain in the north before news reached the Roman commander Stilicho. Pulling his Roman troops out of Gaul and the Rhine border, Stilicho assembled all his reserves to confront Alaric at Pollentia (present-day Piemonte) in 402 CE. Alaric and his forces were defeated and made a hasty withdrawal from Italy.

In 408 CE, the emperor Honorius became suspicious of Stilicho's loyalty and arranged for him to be murdered, which left the emperor without an able general to defend his empire. At the same time, a new political party came to power in Rome. The anti-barbarian party called for the elimination of all the barbarians (foreigners) living within the empire as foederati (federates). One of its first acts was to arrange the massacre of all the families of barbarian troops serving in the Roman army. The Gothic foederati defected to join Alaric, increasing his army to a considerable extent.

The Sack of Rome

Alaric was soon on the move again, laying siege to Rome and demanding supplies and land for his people. Honorius, who had no Stilicho to defend him now, refused to negotiate and withdrew to the fortified city of Ravenna. Eventually, in 410 CE, allies within Rome opened the city's gates to Alaric's forces, who then systematically plundered the capital for three days. Few buildings were destroyed and the citizens were treated humanely, but Honorius's sister, Galla Placidia, was taken hostage.

Alaric died soon after the sack of Rome, while planning to invade Sicily and northern Africa. He was succeeded by his brother, Ataulf. Under Ataulf, the Visigoths left Italy and took up residence in southern Gaul, where the king married Galla Placidia to gain favor with the Romans. However, competing Roman generals who were elected emperor by their troops tended to use Gaul as a base for their campaigns, and one such general drove the Visigoths over the Pyrenees and into Spain. Ataulf died there, in Barcelona, in 415 CE.

The next Visigothic ruler, Wallia, made peace with Rome and sent Galla Placidia back. He fought for the Romans against invading Vandals, and under him, the Visigoths gained control over a great part of Spain. In 418 CE, the Romans called Wallia back to Aquitania, where the Visigoths were accorded the status of foederati. They were assigned places to live and were permitted self-rule in return for military service in the Roman army. Not long after the settlement, Wallia died. He was succeeded by Alaric's son, Theodoric I.

The Visigoths in Spain

Theodoric I ruled the Visigoths from 419 to 451 CE. He was then killed by the Huns during the Battle of the Catalaunian Plains and succeeded by his son Euric, who extended Visigothic territory to

The Beginning of Rome's End

The Battle of Adrianople in 378 CE, in which the Visigothic forces routed the Roman army, is often seen as the beginning of the final downfall of the Roman Empire.

The eastern Roman emperor Valens had allowed Visigoths to settle in his territory as federates, but local Roman governors had continued to harass them. The Goths went on a rampage. Valens decided to confront them in battle and sent a message to the western emperor Gratian, asking for help.

Before Gratian's forces could arrive, however, Valens marched his army of around forty thousand men from Constantinople to Adrianople (present-day Edirne in Turkey). The next day, August 9, he left the camp and advanced around 8 miles (13 km) north, where scouts had located the Gothic forces. After a seven-hour march in difficult conditions, the Romans sighted the Gothic camp set on a low hill. It was a typical Gothic formation called a *laager*, in which their wagons were drawn up in a circle to enclose their families and goods.

The Gothic army numbered around fifty thousand men, but around half were cavalry who were away from camp foraging for supplies. The foot soldiers, under their commander Fritigern, took up position in front of the laager, preparing to defend it. Fritigern set fire to the surrounding fields, hoping the smoke would delay and confuse the Romans. When the Romans attacked, the battle initially seemed to go well for them. However, messengers from the laager had been sent to alert the Gothic cavalry, who now returned and attacked the right flank of the Roman army, driving off the Roman cavalry. The Gothic horsemen then circled around to surround the Roman infantry, whom they cut to pieces. By nightfall, the Romans were in full retreat, and in the rout, Valens himself was killed.

The battle was a disaster for the Romans. Around half the army was killed, including many important officers and administrators. Theodosius I later negotiated a peace with the Visigoths that allowed them to settle in Roman territory on favorable terms.

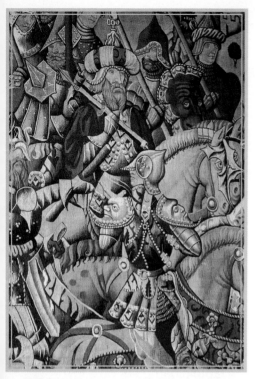

encompass an area from the Pyrenees to the Loire River, as well as most of Spain. In 475 CE, Euric shook off any pretense of dependence on Rome and declared himself king of an independent realm.

In 507 CE, Euric's son Alaric II was defeated at Vouillé by the Frankish king Clovis. As a result, the Visigoths lost almost all their possessions in Aquitania. From that time on, the Visigothic kingdom consisted mainly of most of Spain and a small coastal strip called Septimania, the remnant of their Aquitanian lands.

The Visigoths had been converted to the Arian form of Christianity in the fourth century CE, when they had settled in Moesia. This caused constant conflicts with the orthodox Christians in Romanized areas where they settled. In Spain, the majority of the population was Roman Catholic. It was not until the late sixth century CE that the Visigothic king announced that he would convert to Catholicism to end the continual friction. The two populations became more united, and the Visigothic kingdom enjoyed great prosperity for more than a century.

The Visigoths continued to rule until the early eighth century CE, when they were conquered by Muslims.

The Ostrogoths

The Ostrogothic king **Theodoric the Great**, the son of a chieftain named Theodemir, was born in 454 CE in Pannonia. As a boy, he was sent as a hostage to Constantinople, where he received a Roman education. On the death of his father in 471 CE, he was elected king of the Ostrogoths.

This was a difficult time for the Ostrogoths. They had been driven out of Ukraine by the Huns and sought refuge in Pannonia, but they

King Odoacer

Odoacer was born around 433 CE. His father, Idico, was probably the chief of the Scyrri, one of several Germanic tribes competing for land and food in the Roman provinces of Noricum and Pannonia on the Danube border. When he was around thirty, Odoacer set off for Rome to join the imperial army. Legend recounts that he asked a blessing from a hermit, who told him: "You who are now clad in vile raiment will soon give precious gifts to many." In the Roman army, Odoacer soon rose through the ranks to gain a high position.

In 475 CE, the western emperor Julius Nepos was overthrown by Orestes, a Roman general who then put his fourteen-year-old son on the throne as the emperor **Romulus Augustulus**. However, the tribal mercenaries in the army rejected the titular emperor. Declaring Odoacer to be their king, they captured Orestes and beheaded him. Augustulus was exiled, and Odoacer was accepted by some as the ruler of all Italy. He reigned for thirteen years before being captured and killed by the Gothic leader Theodoric, at the instigation of the eastern emperor Zeno.

found themselves constantly harassed by other marauding Germanic tribes. On becoming king, Theodoric led his people into Moesia, in present-day Bulgaria, but they found it impossible to find land where they could settle in peace. Famine was a constant threat, and even though he tried to maintain good relations with the eastern Roman emperor Zeno, Theodoric often raided Roman provinces to find supplies for his people.

Zeno, eager to get the Ostrogoths on his side, gave Theodoric the title Imperial Master of Soldiers in 483 CE and, in 488 CE, sent him to Italy to overthrow the barbarian ruler Odoacer and then rule on Zeno's behalf.

With an army of perhaps one hundred thousand men, Theodoric entered Italy in 489 CE and, after winning battles at Isonzo, Milan, and Adda, besieged Ravenna. Ravenna held out for three years before it capitulated, and shortly afterward, Theodoric murdered Odoacer and all his family. Declaring himself king of Italy, Theodoric ruled for the next thirty-three years, paying only lip service to the idea that he was a vassal of the eastern emperor.

Under the rule of Theodoric, the country flourished. The military strength of the Ostrogoths brought stability and security, while the Roman aristocracy continued to run the civil administration. For the ordinary Roman populace, life carried on much as before. There were even some new improvements; Theodoric began a program of public works, repairing roads and aqueducts, as well as improving harbors and constructing new buildings.

Theodoric attempted to maintain peaceful relations with his new subjects, constantly urging the Ostrogothic troops to treat the Italian population fairly. Although the Ostrogoths were Arian Christians and the Romans were orthodox Catholics, Theodoric's aim was to live harmoniously with them, and there was no religious persecution. Theodoric died in 526 CE, and the Ostrogothic kingdom in Italy survived for barely a quarter of a century after his death.

The Huns

During the fourth century CE, bands of fierce horsemen from beyond the Volga River began raiding westward into the Danubian provinces. These raiders were the Huns, nomadic tribes whose skills as horsemen and archers enabled them to make sudden raids that inspired terror in local populations. The Huns' raids pushed both the Ostrogoths and the Visigoths west into the Roman Empire, but the Huns kept coming, raiding the eastern empire on small, highly mobile steppe horses.

By 432 CE, the Huns were united under a king called Roas. He negotiated an astute deal with the eastern Roman Empire, obtaining payment of an annual tribute in return for calling off the raids. Roas died in 434 CE, by which time the empire of the Huns extended from the Ural River east as far as the Rhine and from the Danube River north to the Baltic Sea.

Roas was succeeded by his two nephews, **Attila** and **Bleda**, who agreed to rule jointly. They negotiated a new treaty with the eastern Roman Empire (the Treaty of Margus) under which they were to receive double the previous annual tribute and to be given trade rights.

When the Romans reneged on the deal, war broke out, during which the Huns came perilously close to Constantinople. Thoroughly alarmed, the eastern Roman emperor Theodosius II agreed to meet the Huns' demands and signed the Peace of Anatolius in 443 CE. However, once the Huns had retreated, the emperor reneged on the deal again.

Attila the Hun

In 445 CE, Attila murdered his brother and became sole ruler of the Huns. The murder began a career that earned him the nickname "the scourge of God." Two years later, he had conquered the Balkans and Thrace (forcing all the male inhabitants to serve in his army) and was again threatening Constantinople. Theodosius bought off the Huns with an enormous annual tribute and the promise of extensive lands south of the Danube.

Attila turned his attention to Gaul. In 451 CE, he mounted a large-scale invasion in alliance with the Vandals and their king, **Gaiseric**. Attila's troops crossed the Rhine at two points, Koblenz and Basel, and advanced into Gaul, being joined by contingents of **Alans** and Ostrogoths. There was little resistance. The Franks who occupied the banks of the Rhine in the north let the army pass unchallenged. After taking Metz, the Huns continued west to lay siege to Orléans.

The Roman general Flavius Aetius was already in southern Gaul with an army, and he was now ordered by the western Roman emperor Valentinian III to repel Attila. Aware that he could not defeat Attila's army on his own, Aetius sent overtures to Theodoric, king of the Visigoths, and persuaded

Attila the Hun's contemporaries called him the "Scourge of God."

him to join forces with the Romans to confront the Huns. The combined forces of the Romans and the Visigoths moved north to meet Attila in the Catalaunian Plains in 451 CE.

According to legend, Attila summoned his soothsayers to foretell the outcome of the battle. The soothsayers scorched tortoise shells and the shoulder blades of slaughtered sheep and divined from the cracks they found in the scorched items that Attila would be defeated, but that his enemy would die.

The battle was a bloodbath. Contemporary historians estimated Attila's losses at two hundred thousand killed, although that was probably an exaggeration. Attila shot the first arrow, and he fought in the front line throughout the battle, as did Theodoric, king of the Visigoths. At some point, Theodoric was thrown from his horse and killed. Attila's enemy had indeed died, as prophesied, but it was not Aetius. Toward evening, Roman charges forced the Huns to retreat, with the Visigoths in close pursuit.

The following day, to everyone's amazement and for reasons that are still not entirely understood, Aetius asked the Goths to withdraw, leaving Attila to retreat from Gaul unhindered. It may be that Aetius feared the threat that the Visigoths themselves might present to Rome if the Huns were entirely defeated.

Attila's Italian Campaign

Attila recovered quickly and, setting his sights on Rome itself, crossed the Alps to the Po Plain of Italy. He besieged and sacked Aquileia, and other cities of northern Italy paid tribute to him to avoid devastation. Before he could reach Rome, emissaries (including Pope Leo I) were sent out to intercede with him. Exactly what took place in the meeting is not known, but it may be that the Romans offered Attila considerable cash to withdraw. With disease and famine rife in his army, he may have felt that discretion was the better part of valor. In any case, after the conference, Attila marched his army out of Italy. "Attila, thou art the most mighty conqueror," Pope Leo is said to have told him. "Thou hast conquered thyself."

Attila returned to the Balkans. He then planned another attack on Constantinople because the new eastern Roman emperor Marcian had stopped paying tribute. In 453 CE, Attila married a German princess called Ildico, but during the wedding night, he died from what appeared to be a massive hemorrhage from the nose.

The empire that Attila had built up did not long outlast his death. Although his eldest son, Ellac, succeeded him, his other two sons fought over the inheritance. Seeing the empire falling apart from the top, many of the subjugated tribes rebelled. In 455 CE, an alliance of Germanic peoples defeated the Huns at the Battle of Nedao. Fourteen years later, Dengizich, the last king of the Huns, was defeated by Roman and Gothic forces, marking the end of the empire.

The Vandals

The Vandals were among the first Germanic peoples to migrate to the region of the Danube River. Originally from Jutland (part of present-day Denmark), the Vandals settled along the Danube in the second and third centuries CE, moving to the valley of the Oder River in the fourth century CE. Early in the fifth century CE, they entered Gaul under their king Godigisel and were met in battle by the Franks in 406 CE. Godigisel was killed, along with twenty thousand Vandals, but the Franks were defeated. Under Godigisel's son Gunderic, the Vandals continued westward.

In 409 CE, the Vandals reached Spain and established a kingdom, having received land from the Romans and permission to settle as federates. Gunderic died in 428 CE and was succeeded by his half-brother, Gaiseric. Gaiseric, probably the greatest of the Vandal kings, started building a fleet of ships. In 429 CE, with around eighty thousand men, he sailed across the Strait of Gibraltar and landed in northern Africa, which was then a province of the Romans.

Gaiseric soon conquered much of what is now Morocco and Algeria, forcing the Roman commander Bonifacius to flee to Italy. By 435 CE, the Vandals had seized most of the coastal strip, but with their basic fighting tactics, they found it hard to capture the major cities. Not until 439 CE, ten years after their arrival, were the Vandals able to capture Carthage. According to one story, the Vandals took the city without a fight when the citizens were all at the races. Gaiseric

The Vandals sacked Rome in 455 CE.

The Fall of Rome and the Rise of Constantinople

established a capital at Carthage, and the independence of the Vandal kingdom in northern Africa was recognized by the western Roman emperor Valentinian III in 440 CE.

The new rulers of northern Africa were skilled seamen, and with their large fleet of ships, they proceeded to dominate the Mediterranean. They plundered the coasts of the eastern and western Roman empires and captured the islands of Sicily, Sardinia, and Corsica. In 455 CE, the emperor Valentinian III died, and Gaiseric seized the chance to attack Rome itself. This time, the negotiations of Leo I were unable to prevent the city from being sacked, although Gaiseric agreed to spare civilian lives. The Vandals entered the city unopposed and plundered it for two weeks, carrying away anything of value, including the empress Eudoxia and her two daughters as hostages and many Roman citizens as slaves.

The triumphant Gaiseric and his forces moved east, heading for Constantinople. En route, they pillaged in Greece and Dalmatia. The western Roman emperor Majorian tried to stop them in 457 CE, as did the eastern emperor Leo I in 468 CE, but both were unsuccessful. Finally, in 476 CE, the eastern emperor Zeno made peace with the Vandals. Gaiseric died the following year and was succeeded by his son Hunneric, who reigned from 477 to 484 CE.

The Vandals were Arian Christians and were theologically opposed to the orthodox Christianity of their subjugated peoples. In Africa, they persecuted the Catholics fiercely, exiling the bishops and confiscating the property of Catholic citizens. As the power of the Vandals began to disintegrate after the death of Gaiseric, this persecution provided a spur for the armies of the eastern Roman Empire to recover former possessions. In 533 CE, the Byzantine emperor Justinian I declared war on the Vandals. Their empire was finally brought down in 534 CE by the Byzantine general **Belisarius**.

The Franks

A Germanic people called the Franks had originally established themselves along the Rhine River in the third century CE. One group, known as the Salian Franks, invaded Roman territory in the mid-fourth century CE. Although they were driven back in 358 CE by the future Roman emperor Julian, they had gained part of what is present-day Belgium. Subsequently, some of these Franks were accepted into the Roman army as federates and helped to defend the frontier. In 402 CE, when the Roman general Stilicho withdrew his troops from the Rhine in order to stop the Visigoths' invasion of Italy, the Salians took over the region, establishing a small kingdom on the outer edge of the disintegrating Roman Empire. They led a traditional Germanic life, worshipping the gods of the sun and thunder (Wodan and Freya) and barely being touched by cultural influences from the south.

By the fifth century CE, a Frankish center of power had grown up in Tournai and was ruled by a king named Childeric I. Little is known of him, apart from the fact that he died in 481 CE and was succeeded by his fifteen-year-old son Chlodowech, known to history as **Clovis I**. Clovis is regarded as the first important ruler of the Merovingian dynasty, which was named after Merovich, his grandfather. Clovis was energetic in expanding his kingdom through conquest, treachery, and murder. In 486 CE, he marched on the city of Soissons (northeast of Paris), captured the city, and seized all the holdings of the Roman Empire in Gaul from its governor Syagrius.

Clovis's Conversion

In 493 CE, Clovis married **Clotilda**, the orthodox Christian daughter of a prince of Burgundy (see sidebar, page 85).

Three years later, he confronted the army of the Alemanni, a Germanic tribe established along the upper courses of the Rhine. According to legend, when the battle seemed to be going against him, Clovis called upon his wife's god to help. Clovis promised that, if God would grant him victory, he would be baptized. The tide of battle turned, Clovis was victorious, and later that year, he converted to Catholic Christianity. He was baptized in Reims, together with important members of his court. His conversion made him popular far beyond the reaches of his Frankish followers.

Clovis's conversion proved to be an astute political move. Most of his fellow barbarian overlords in Europe were Arian Christians, which put them at odds with the Catholic Roman populations they had conquered. By becoming a Catholic, Clovis won the loyalty of

St. Clotilda, Queen of the Franks

Clotilda was born in 474 CE. She was the daughter of Chilperic (a son of the king of Burgundy) and his Roman wife Caretena. Clotilda grew up in her mother's Catholic faith. While she was still a teenager, Clotilda was initiated into the harsh realities of the world at that time. Both her parents were killed by her uncle, Gundobad, and her sister was exiled.

Clotilda was beautiful and intelligent, and her uncle may have hoped to arrange a marriage for her that would be advantageous to him. Clotilda had other ideas, however. When Clovis, the powerful king of the Franks, heard of the beauty of the princess, he sent an envoy to woo her secretly, presenting her with a gold ring and other gifts. Clotilda accepted the proposal. Clovis then formally asked her uncle for Clotilda in marriage, and Gundobad dared not refuse. The couple married in 493 CE in Soissons, when Clotilda was not yet twenty years old.

Clotilda soon acquired great influence over her husband, and he allowed their first two sons to be baptized. The first son died in infancy, which would have seemed to be a bad omen for Clotilda's god. Nevertheless, Clovis himself converted to Christianity three years later, after he called on his wife's god to help him in a battle that he subsequently won. Thereafter, the Frankish kingdom became a leader of Catholic Christianity in the west.

Clotilda bore Clovis three more children before he died in 511 CE. She then retired to a convent in Tours, where she earned a reputation for holiness and good works. She died in 545 CE. Shortly after her death, Clotilda was canonized.

After his victory at the Battle of Tolbiac in 496 CE, Clovis made good on his vow to be baptized into the Catholic faith.

his Roman subjects, laying the basis for a close-knit empire. The conversion enabled Clovis to adopt the guise of religious liberator in all further wars he fought, and it gained him the support of the Catholic Church for his campaigns. In the following century, Gregory, bishop of Tours, wrote a history of the Franks in which he described Clovis as a ruler who "walked before God with an upright heart and did what was pleasing in his sight." Modern historians, in contrast, often see Clovis as an ambitious ruler who was prepared to act ruthlessly for his own advantage.

By 506 CE, Clovis had subdued the Alemanni. He then killed the Visigothic king Alaric II in battle at Vouillé in 507 CE. Clovis subsequently pushed the Visigoths back over the Pyrenees, reducing their territory outside of Spain to Septimania, a narrow coastal strip between the Pyrenees and the Rhone River. Clovis was now master of Gaul. When he died in 511 CE, he was the undisputed ruler of a Frankish kingdom that stretched from the Rhine to the Pyrenees and from the Main River to the Atlantic. His descendants ruled this kingdom until the eighth century CE, and the name "Frank" gave the region its present-day name of "France."

These reliefs of battle are from a sarcophagus belonging to a Roman general who fought in the Germanic campaigns under Marcus Aurelius.

CHAPTER SEVEN

Life Under the Barbarians

For many former citizens of the Roman Empire, the change in imperial rulers made little difference. In spite of their reputation among the Romans, the Germanic barbarians had well-developed cultures and ideas of social and political organization.

Although the western Roman Empire fell to Germanic invaders over the course of the fourth and fifth centuries CE, Roman culture was not destroyed. This was in part a matter of numbers. The invaders were few, while the former Roman citizens were many. The conquering tribes took control of government, but they did not dominate society.

In part, too, the invaders did not want to overthrow Roman achievements. The signs of the civilization they had overrun made an overwhelming impression on the invaders. Even though their own cultures were ancient, they were not technically advanced. The newcomers marveled at Rome's temples, the now empty *insulae* (public apartment houses), and the ruined aqueducts built by earlier generations. None of the Germanic tribes had writing, so they were limited to knowledge passed on by oral tradition. They were awestruck by Roman art, science, and literature and tried to learn from them. The invaders were just as impressed by the well-organized Roman bureaucracy, with high officials distinguished by the trappings of office.

Germanic Religion and Culture

The invading armies needed places to live. In order to obtain accommodation for their troops, the Germanic tribes invoked an old

Roman custom, *hospitium* (visitor's rights). This custom placed an obligation on the residents of a district to offer hospitality to travelers, but it soon became little more than a euphemism for billeting soldiers. All local landowners were required to provide housing for the foreign invaders, who, for military reasons, preferred to live close together rather than be dispersed throughout the territories they controlled.

As a rule, the Germanic invaders made no attempt to integrate with local populations. Nor did they try to change the law, the distribution of wealth, or the official hierarchy of conquered areas. They settled down among the original inhabitants and led their own lives according to the traditions they brought with them across the Rhine and Danube rivers. Only at the apex of society, with the king, did the two parallel lives converge. The monarch had sole authority over the entire government.

For most of the Roman population, little changed, barring the presence of a rarely seen royal tax collector. That was not the case, however, with religion. Most of the Germanic invaders followed Arian Christianity, while orthodox Catholicism prevailed among the Romans. This difference lessened any loyalty the Romans may have felt to their new masters.

Most of the invaders did not interfere with their subjects' faith, but the Vandals persecuted orthodox Christians. It was not until the sixth century CE that the religious difference was bridged. At that point in time, both the Franks and the Visigoths embraced Catholicism.

Reorganizing Power

By the fifth century CE, although many Goths had been given the status of federates of the Romans and served as soldiers to defend the empire in return for land or other concessions, they knew that real power lay with their own leaders. Both the emperors and the tribal chiefs knew that the central authority of Rome was at an end.

The political structure that the Germanic tribes brought into the former empire did undergo major changes as they gained power. Whereas once they had distributed land annually to their members on the basis of social class, they now suddenly found themselves in possession of vast areas. The Visigoths controlled much of what is now Spain and southern France, the **Lombards** held the greater part of

Preserving Ancient Culture

The survival of knowledge of the works of the Greek philosophers Plato and Aristotle, together with the works of other ancient writers, is owed largely to two Roman scholars of the fifth and sixth centuries CE.

A woodcut of the Roman philosopher Boethius, ca. 1754 CE

The first of these scholars was Boethius (ca. 480–534 CE). The son of a Roman consul, Boethius held the highly respected position of *magister officiorum* in the court of Theodoric, the Ostrogothic ruler of Italy. Boethius was fluent in Greek at a time when the language was falling into disuse, and he set out to translate into Latin the works of Plato and Aristotle, at the same time writing extensive commentaries on them. Before he could complete his task, he was thrown into prison on a charge of treason. While awaiting execution, he wrote *Consolation of Philosophy*, a work based on the main beliefs of Platonism. Boethius's book was read extensively in the Middle Ages, and it kept Plato's ideas alive at a time when pagan writers were largely frowned on by the church.

The second scholar was **Cassiodorus** (ca. 490–583 CE), who replaced Boethius at Theodoric's court. After Cassiodorus retired, he founded a monastery dedicated to preserving classical culture. He collected manuscripts and drew up a kind of reading list that included the works of Boethius. He encouraged his monks to make copies of ancient works, both Christian and pagan, establishing a tradition that was followed in later monasteries.

Italy, and the Vandals ruled the Mediterranean and the former Roman province of Africa. It was obvious that something had to change.

Back in 98 CE, the Roman historian Tacitus, in his treatise Germania, had described how Germanic society was organized. He noted that their society was based on the *pagus* (clan), each of which selected a chief whose power was limited by the tribal council and the *comitium* (a group of warriors who swore allegiance to the chief). By the fourth century CE, however, the clan meeting no longer served as a decision-making body, and authority had shifted to a single king. The king was chosen by members of his bloodline, and his most important function was to serve as commander of the army. Those who performed well, such as Alaric and Theodoric, rose to great power. Their new subjects, former Roman citizens, were accustomed to a single powerful leader and readily followed the conquerors.

Whereas most of the Germanic tribes had originally been nomadic or at least accustomed to moving from place to place in search of new lands, tribal kings now began to rule from a fixed place of residence, following the model of the Roman court. Each king assembled a group of officials to take care of administration. Each king also appointed a *major domus* (chief official of the palace) to manage the royal household. This official eventually acquired great influence—more than that of the ministers and judges of the Roman administration.

Germanic Law

Once the Germanic empires were established on Roman soil, their kings—again following Roman example—attempted to record their traditional laws in writing. Germanic law was characterized by two things: trial by ordeal and blood money. Almost all crimes were punishable by fines, and divine judgment was invoked to determine the guilt or innocence of the accused.

Trial by fire or heat was common. Suspected criminals were made to grip a red-hot poker, walk barefoot over burning coals, or reach into boiling water to retrieve a stone. Those whose injuries healed well were presumed to be innocent, while those whose injuries became infected were pronounced guilty. Sometimes, it was the accuser rather than the accused who had to undergo trial by ordeal. If a Lombard man accused a woman of being a witch, he had to prove himself in a ritual fight called a *kampfio*.

For people of high rank who were accused of a crime, the verdict might be reached by an oath-taking ceremony, called *compugation*. The accused had to assemble a number of witnesses known as "oath helpers." These witnesses would observe the accused swear an oath that he was innocent, and then they would in turn swear their own oath that he was telling the truth.

When an accused person was found guilty, the punishment was in nearly all cases a fine. The Germanic peoples held to the concept of blood money, assigning a specific value to everyone according to rank. If someone injured or killed another person, he had to pay the appropriate blood money to the injured party or to the injured party's relatives. Under Frankish law, for example, a blow to the head that fractured the skull and exposed the brain would cost

This statue of the historian Tacitus stands in front of the Austrian Parliament, Vienna.

thirty solidi, while under Lombard law, "for blows to the head that cause a fracture of the base of the skull, one must pay twelve solidi for each bone."

Other fines specified under Lombard law included that for putting out a person's eye or chopping off his nose (six solidi), while each front tooth was worth seventeen solidi, and each molar was worth half of that. Killing a pregnant woman incurred a fine four times that for killing a freeman. The Lombard legislator explained: "For all of these injuries and fights that can occur between freemen, we have arranged settlements that are more liberal than those our ancestors applied, so there will be an end to the blood feud, and so that one will bear no grudges, but instead those who had been enemies can live as friends."

Blood money differed from one tribe to another, and in some cases, even insults were punishable by a fine. Calling someone a "sly fox" or a "hare" incurred a fine of three denarii, while accusing someone of being a liar cost fifteen.

Physical punishment was generally reserved for slaves because they had no property or money. If a slave stole something small, the law sentenced him to 120 blows, but if he stole a larger amount, he could be castrated.

The principle behind all Germanic laws was that of compensating the victim of a crime. This differed radically from Roman law, whose goal was punishment of the criminal. Roman law did not entirely die out under Germanic rule. A version survived among the vanquished population, and in later centuries, Roman jurisprudence would become the basis of many justice systems.

The Barbarian Family

The ties of clan and kinship were integral to Germanic legal principles. For example, under Frankish law, anyone who was unable to pay his debts could transfer them to his closest relative. To do this, he had to swear that he had nothing "upon the earth or under," collect a handful of dust from the corners of his hut, throw it on his closest relative, and then jump over his fence. He was then declared insolvent, and his family became responsible for the payment of his debts.

It was also possible to separate oneself from the family. The individual had to appear before witnesses, break four elm branches over his head, and throw them in all four directions. This ceremony broke all ties with his family, including any obligations incurred by blood feud or blood money.

Women had virtually no legal rights. The Germanic concept of family included the man's right of possession (*mundium*) over his wife and any other women he had, his children, his slaves, and his freemen.

Britannia

During the fourth century CE, the province of Britain was not a major concern of the Roman Empire. The imperial government had other priorities. Rome itself was under threat, and people in the other parts of the empire were being plundered by roaming bands of invading tribes. From the beginning of the fifth century CE, however, marauding groups from Scandinavia descended on the coast of Britain, making lightning raids in their oceangoing ships.

Depending on the source, authors hold that King Arthur's Round Table could fit between 50 and 1,600 men.

When the Visigoths invaded Italy in 402 CE, the last Roman garrison was recalled from Britain to assist in Rome's defense. The British-Roman population in the island was left without any military defense, and in the north, the Picts and Scots raided the countryside unchecked. They breached the Antonine Wall and, farther south, Hadrian's Wall, both built by the Romans more than two hundred years earlier. The Britons sent a cry for help to Rome, but it was ignored. Rome had abandoned the province.

The Angles, Saxons, and Jutes invaded and settled in Britain during the fifth century CE, and many Britons fled across the English Channel to take refuge in the Roman province of Armorica, which was located in northwestern Gaul. The region would become known as Brittany after these Britons, who largely retained their own language and customs.

It took the Angles and Saxons more than a century to establish a dominant culture in Britain. Around 500 CE, they were confronted and defeated in battle by a local chieftain called Artorius, the historical figure on whom the legendary King Arthur is thought to have been based.

This was similar to the Roman concept of possession called *manus*. Under Frankish law, a woman could not inherit land, while the law of the Lombards stated: "It is illegal for a free woman to live according to her own will because she always continues to be subject to the power of a man, whether husband or relative. Therefore she cannot transfer her property, movable or immovable, without the permission of the person under whose mundium she lives."

The laws relating to marriage and inheritance were very specific. It was the custom among the Germanic peoples for the husband to give his wife a "morning gift" on the morning after their wedding night, and the wife was expected to give the husband a dowry, called the "father's money." Under Lombard law, careful arrangements were made for the distribution of property after the dissolution of a marriage, the death of either spouse, or a second marriage. Illegitimate children had a right to at least a portion of the inheritance, and disinheriting children was not permitted. The property of anyone who died childless passed to the king. In order to prevent this, people who had no successors would give away their land while they were still alive.

On marriage, the wife came under the mundium of her husband, and if he died, of the eldest son. If the widow had no son, she went back to the mundium of her family. If she had no family, the king appointed a guardian who was legally obliged to defend her if she was falsely accused of a crime.

Language and the Decline of Civilization

Closer contact between the people and their Germanic rulers eventually had an effect on language. The modern languages of Iceland, Scandinavia, England, and Germany all derive from the original Indo-European languages of the Germanic tribes. Latin became vulgarized as local people adapted it. Regional variations grew apart over the centuries, becoming eventually the Romance languages: Italian, French, and Spanish.

Commerce declined. The Germanic rulers had little interest in economic development or trade. They were farmers who valued mainly land; their communities were self-sufficient, and trade was very limited. The circulation of money virtually ceased. Kings occasionally minted gold

An alliance of Germans annihilated three Roman legions at the Battle of Teutoburg Forest in 9 CE.

A Pictish craftsman carved symbols into this stone located in Scotland, United Kingdom. Peoples such as the Picts were never incorporated into the Roman Empire.

coins, but the coins were seldom taken out of the treasury. Europe had returned to being an agrarian society.

Most cities were abandoned, and engineering projects were halted. In Rome, ancient monuments were demolished for stone, and the forum became a meadow. Aqueducts collapsed, and floods turned the area outside Rome into a swamp.

Cultural knowledge from Roman and Greek times was preserved only in Europe's monasteries (see sidebar, page 91). Latin became largely a written language, learned only by priests and monks. Ordinary people spoke other languages and were illiterate. Even the Germanic kings never learned to read and write.

Planning to Restore the Empire

While the western Roman Empire was being taken over by Germanic peoples, an eastern, or Byzantine, emperor still reigned at Constantinople. At the end of the fifth century CE, the Byzantine throne was reasonably secure. The state was defended by an army, the bureaucracy functioned reasonably well, and the rule of the emperors was largely uncontested. The Byzantine rulers never lost their interest in the west. Still hoping to win back the lost western territories, diplomats played the Germanic kings against each other. By the sixth century CE, the east was gathering its forces to re-conquer the west.

This sixth-century CE mosaic of Justinian I is from the Basilica of San Vitale, in Ravenna, Italy.

CHAPTER EIGHT

Emperor Justinian

In the late fifth century CE, while the western Roman Empire collapsed under barbarian invasions, the eastern Roman Empire enjoyed relative stability. One of its most notable rulers was Justinian I, who is famous for the legal code he established.

Before the emperor Theodosius I died in January of 395 CE, he decreed that the Roman Empire should be divided after his death. His twelve-year-old son Honorius was to become emperor in the west, while his eighteen-year-old son Arcadius would assume power in the east.

Early Eastern Emperors

Theodosius appointed the loyal and capable general Flavius Stilicho as regent for Honorius, and this move stabilized the western empire. In the east, however, Arcadius proved to be a weak and ineffectual ruler. The court at Constantinople was riddled with intrigue, and no strong leader emerged from the many ambitious and unscrupulous contenders for power. Two contenders who had the greatest influence on Arcadius were Rufinus, the Praetorian prefect, and Eutropius, a eunuch and former slave. Arcadius was also very much under the influence of his wife, Eudoxia (see sidebar, page 103).

Arcadius died at age thirty-one in May of 408 CE, and he was succeeded by his son, Theodosius II, who was only seven years old. For several years, power remained in the hands of a corrupt court clique of eunuchs, ministers, prelates, and princesses, who ran the empire for their own profit. The only exception was the pious Pulcheria, the emperor's elder sister. In 414 CE, when she was fifteen years old, Pulcheria was made Augusta (empress), and her influence remained considerable for the next thirty-six years. When Theodosius fell from his horse and died in 450 CE, the choice of a successor was left to Pulcheria. The man she chose was a senator and former officer named Marcian, whom she married pro forma (in name only) in order to preserve the dynasty of Theodosius.

The eastern Roman (or Byzantine) Empire managed to survive the tempestuous years of the early fifth century CE relatively unscathed. Since 397 CE, when the Visigothic king Alaric had signed a peace treaty with Arcadius, no one had presented a serious threat to the eastern empire. The stream of migrating Goths and Huns flowed mainly west, and those tribes that did spill into the eastern empire were primarily interested in spoils and could usually be bought off. Some immigrants were permitted to enter the empire at the Danube border, and Marcian gave the Ostrogoths land in Pannonia. While the traditional enemy, Persia, continued to be a threat, it was less aggressive in the fifth century CE than in the past.

Marcian died in 457 CE and was replaced by Leo I. Leo's reign, which lasted until 474 CE, was most noted for a disastrous campaign against the Vandals in Africa, which almost bankrupted the eastern empire. Leo I was succeeded by his grandson Leo II, who outlived him by only a few months.

The next emperor was Zeno, son-in-law of Leo I and father of Leo II. Zeno was born in Isauria (a region of present-day Turkey) and had risen to prominence in the army of Leo I. Zeno's reign was marked by a number of revolts and uprisings. The most significant rebellion was instigated by the Ostrogoths that Marcian had allowed to settle in Pannonia. The Ostrogoths, led by their king Theodoric, had begun to cause problems in the Balkans. In 488 CE, Zeno persuaded the Ostrogothic king to relocate his people to Italy, where he would overthrow the barbarian Odoacer and rule the country with the recognition of the eastern emperor.

On Zeno's death in 491 CE, his widow, Ariadne, arranged for a senior palace official named Anastasius to replace him as both the emperor and her husband. During Anastasius's reign, the empire went to war with both the Isaurians and the Sassanid Persians.

Empress Eudoxia

Eudoxia was the daughter of a Frankish chieftain who had been a Roman consul for a term in 385 CE. She was extremely beautiful, a fact noted by the eunuch Eutropius when he was casting about for a way to thwart his rival Rufinus. Knowing that Rufinus planned to marry his daughter to Arcadius, Eutropius brought Eudoxia to the court. She swiftly caught the eye of the new emperor, and they were married in April of 395 CE.

Eudoxia enjoyed her new position and exploited it to the hilt. Her court became notorious for its extravagance and depravity, and she came to resent the power that Eutropius seemed to think he had over her. In 399 CE, Gainas, then head of the army of the east, demanded the surrender of Eutropius to appease insurgents in Phrygia. Eudoxia persuaded the emperor to accede to these terms, and Eutropius's fate was sealed.

The excesses of her court and lifestyle brought Eudoxia into conflict with the bishop of Constantinople, John Chrysostom. He condemned the empress and her circle so roundly that Eudoxia schemed to have him exiled. In 404 CE, she succeeded in having him expelled from Constantinople, and he died in Armenia in 407 CE.

Eudoxia bore Arcadius four daughters and a son, Theodosius, who later became emperor. Eudoxia died in October of 404 CE.

Justinian I Becomes Emperor

When Anastasius died in 518 CE, he was succeeded by Justin, the commander of the palace guard. Coming from peasant stock, the new emperor was uneducated and in his middle sixties—hardly promising material for his exalted position. However, he had one enormous advantage—a young nephew called Justinian, who was everything Justin was not. Justinian had been educated in Constantinople and, at the time of his uncle's accession, was an officer in one of the royal regiments.

After becoming emperor, Justin legally adopted his nephew and came to rely heavily on him for advice in matters of state. In April of

The Nika Revolt

The Nika revolt began as an angry mob during one of the horse races at the Hippodrome.

In the early years of his reign, Justinian relied heavily upon two officials—the Praetorian prefect John of Cappadocia (who supervised all tax collection) and the quaestor Tribonian (who was responsible for administering justice). Both men were extremely unpopular with the people at large. Discontent grew to such an extent that the Green and Blue parties, who were usually bitter enemies, became united in opposition to the government.

On January 13, 532 CE, the crowd in the Hippodrome started shouting with one voice: *"Nika! Nika!"* ("Victory! Victory!"). This chant was the traditional cry usually hurled by the opposing parties at each other. What had been the call of the racetrack became the battle cry of a rebel movement. As the mob got out of hand, the games were abandoned, and the throng poured out of the arena in an ugly mood. The rebels began to set fire to public buildings, including the great church Hagia Sophia, which was burned to the ground.

The next day, Justinian confronted the mob in the Hippodrome. The dissidents demanded that the city prefect and the two hated ministers be dismissed. Justinian decided that the best way out of the situation was to accede to these demands, and he announced that he would do as the dissidents wished. Unfortunately, this move had precisely the opposite effect from what he had hoped.

The following day in the Hippodrome, elated by their success, the rebels demanded Justinian's resignation. Amid loud cheering, they acclaimed Hypatius, an elderly nephew of the former emperor Anastasius, as their new emperor. Justinian retired hurriedly to his palace.

In the palace, the shaken Justinian consulted with his ministers. All of them were of the opinion that Justinian should make his escape while it was still possible. He could leave the palace by a back door and descend, unseen, to a boat moored in the harbor. However, the empress Theodora, who was horrified by the cowardly plan, succeeded in persuading her husband to stand his ground.

After hearing a report that the masses in the Hippodrome were in disagreement with one another, Justinian decided to risk military action. Two generals took their forces by secret routes to the Hippodrome and fell upon the rebels, cutting them down without mercy. Any rebels who attempted to escape were slaughtered at the exits. Around thirty thousand people were massacred. Hypatius was executed the following day. The Nika Revolt was at an end.

527 CE, the aging emperor made Justinian co-emperor, and when Justin died a few months later, Justinian became the sole emperor.

Justinian had huge ambitions, which were matched by a boundless energy for carrying them out. He had ideas of reuniting the fragmented empire, planning to restore to Roman sovereignty the western provinces taken by Germanic invaders over the past century and reduce the Germanic kingdoms to subordinate status. In his view, a reunited empire was not just politically desirable but a religious necessity.

Christianity, since the fourth century CE, had been inseparably connected with the empire. As far as Justinian was concerned, there could be only one God and only one emperor. His slogan, "One empire, one law, one church," dictated the policy of his government. Throughout his reign, he attempted, without success, to reconcile the doctrinal differences between the Monophysites (who believed that Christ had only one nature) and the theologians of the orthodox church. Despite his efforts, the Monophysites refused to entertain any compromise and even went so far as to organize their own clandestine church in the eastern provinces of Justinian's empire.

Justinian worked day and night both on legislation and on the writing of theological tracts. However, laws and tracts were not enough to achieve his aims—the goal of a united empire demanded both military action abroad and the suppression of dissent at home. Justinian left both these tasks largely to his general Belisarius. However, Justinian's wife was also permitted a significant voice in matters of government.

Justinian married **Theodora** (see sidebar, page 111) in 525 CE. When he became emperor in 527 CE, she was crowned empress and joint ruler with him. Justinian flouted all rules of convention by marrying Theodora, who had been both an actress and a courtesan, but she proved to be a great help to him; she was highly intelligent and had a clear understanding of politics. In 532 CE, when the rebellion called the **Nika Revolt** broke out on the streets of Constantinople, Theodora persuaded the emperor to stand his ground and take decisive action to quell the insurrection.

Peace with Persia

The same year that the Nika Revolt was quashed, the eastern border of the empire was rendered safe by a peace treaty with Persia. Ever since Justinian had taken the throne, his generals had been fighting the Persian king Kavadh I in campaigns that had been, for the most part, successful. On the death of Kavadh, Justinian was able to negotiate a treaty with his successor, **Khosrow I**.

Under the terms of the agreement, the Persian king recognized the Byzantine emperor's right to the lands he occupied in the east. In return, Justinian had to pay a subsidy of eleven thousand pounds of gold. This Treaty of Eternal Peace freed Justinian's forces to fight on other fronts.

The Campaign in Africa

In northern Africa, the former Roman citizens, who were orthodox Christians, had been living under the rule of Arian Vandals. When the Vandal king Hilderich, who had been tolerant of the religious beliefs of the Romans, was deposed by the anti-Roman Gelimer, Justinian decided he must deliver the Roman population from the Vandal overlords. In June of 533 CE, Justinian dispatched an expeditionary force consisting of around five thousand cavalry and ten thousand foot soldiers and commanded by the general Belisarius.

The army landed unopposed on the African coast, marched toward Carthage, and encountered Gelimer and his forces 10 miles (16 km) outside the city. The Vandal army was no match for the Byzantines. The Byzantine cavalry (made up largely of Huns) bore down on the Vandals with horrifying ferocity, and those Vandals who were not cut down turned tail and fled. Two days later, Belisarius entered Carthage in triumph.

The Vandals proved to be without support in the region. The farmers were not interested in warfare, while the city dwellers openly welcomed the Byzantines. In Carthage, orthodox clergymen took over the churches, while the celebrating populace illuminated the town ramparts. The citizens greeted the imperial troops as liberators, and in the palace, Belisarius greeted the city's important officials before holding a feast.

Within a year, all Vandal resistance was at an end. The Vandal kingdom in northern Africa was reincorporated into the empire in 534 CE. Gelimer was finally captured and taken back to Constantinople, where Belisarius was given a triumphant parade in the Hippodrome. Gelimer was forced to prostrate himself before Justinian while the crowd cheered.

A view of the ornamental ceiling of the Hagia Sophia from the ground illustrates its architectural and artistic excellence.

Hagia Sophia

Hagia Sophia, the Church of Holy Wisdom, is Justinian's most lasting monument. It has endured for almost 1,500 years, surviving all kinds of disasters. To this day, its great dome rises above the skyline of Istanbul. The first Hagia Sophia was built by Constantine in the fourth century CE, but it was burned to the ground during the Nika Revolt in 532 CE. Rather than attempting to restore the original church, Justinian decided to build a new, larger church to the glory of God, the empire, and himself.

Justinian commissioned two distinguished architects, Anthemius of Tralles and Isidorus of Miletus, to design a building whose magnificence would be worthy of his aspirations. After researching all prior building techniques, they came up with a revolutionary design of a square (rather than rectangular) base topped by a huge central dome 185 feet (56 m) high. The dome was supported by four massive arches standing on the square base of the structure. Such a transition between dome and base had never been attempted before and represented a major innovation in architecture. At the base of the dome was a circle of forty windows. Because the supports could only be seen on the outside of the building, the windows gave the impression that the dome was floating on a halo of light.

The interior of the church was lit with golden lamps that shone on the exquisite mosaics and decorations of polished marble, while the precious gemstones that encrusted the altar made it blaze with mysterious light. It is little wonder that when he first entered the completed building, Justinian exclaimed: "Solomon, I have outdone thee" (a reference to the temple built by Solomon in Jerusalem).

Some twenty years after the church was completed, the dome collapsed during an earthquake. Justinian ordered new calculations to be made and a sturdier dome to be built. That dome, dating from 563 CE, still graces the church today.

The church survived when the city fell to the Crusaders in 1204 CE and the Ottomans in 1453 CE. The latter converted Hagia Sophia into a mosque. It is now a museum.

However, instead of being executed, Gelimer was given an estate in Galatia, where he lived out his days in retirement.

The Campaign in Italy

Justinian's attention now turned to Italy. Following the death of the Ostrogothic king Theodoric in 526 CE, there was a dynastic struggle for power among his survivors, and Justinian seized the opportunity to make a play for Italy. In 535 CE, Belisarius was dispatched to Sicily with a force of 7,500 men. He took over the island without a fight and then proceeded to attack the Ostrogoths who occupied the Italian mainland.

For the next twenty years, Italy was ravaged by ongoing warfare. What had been presented by Constantinople as a battle of liberation ended in senseless violence, tyranny, and exploitation. The constant fighting eventually took its toll on army discipline, and the Byzantine soldiers were feared everywhere, while the governors were despised and the officials were scorned.

Rome was occupied first by one side and then by the other. When the Goths retreated from Rome, the city was occupied by the

Today, Rome's once great forum lies in ruins. Many of Rome's most impressive buildings were destroyed in the barbarian invasions of the late fifth century CE.

Empress Theodora

The empress Theodora, who lived from around 497 to 548 CE, came from the lowest ranks of society. Her father was a bear tamer in the Hippodrome. The people of Constantinople had low regard for anyone who earned a living by providing some kind of entertainment. The acting profession as a whole was seen as immoral, and little differentiation was made between actresses and prostitutes.

As an adult, Theodora learned the only trade open to her—that of acting. She had both beauty and brains, and she became well known for her performances in risqué roles, such as that of Leda, to whom Zeus made love in the guise of a swan. Theodora acquired throngs of admirers, and her first step into the world of the elite came when a high official took her as his mistress. Moving in powerful circles, Theodora then met Justinian, who was at that time the heir to the throne. It was love at first sight, but the law prevented the marriage of a future emperor to an actress.

However, this legislation proved to be no serious obstacle. Justinian was able to persuade his uncle, Justin I, to rescind the law. A short time later, in 525 CE, Justinian and Theodora were married by the patriarch of Constantinople. Two years later, Justinian was crowned emperor, and Theodora became his empress, acquiring the title of Augusta.

Theodora was around fifteen years younger than her husband. However, from the start, she exercised a strong influence over him. This influence resulted in laws improving the lot of women, particularly in the area of divorce. Theodora also helped to set up a charity that provided a refuge for former prostitutes. The most famous example of her influence over the emperor came during the Nika Revolt, when she persuaded him to stand his ground and confront the rebels.

Byzantines, who were then besieged there for a year by the Goths. Outside the city, the Goths blocked the water supply by destroying the ancient aqueducts, and the famous baths ran dry. Eventually, with their army decimated by the plague, the Goths raised the siege, retreating northward, and the tide swung in favor of the Byzantines once more.

In 540 CE, after Belisarius had taken Ravenna, it appeared that Gothic resistance was at an end. Within a year, however, Italy was again ablaze. The "liberated" Romans had come to loathe the new regime, with its hordes of corrupt officials who swarmed over the country backed up by a rapacious army. These officials included the financial minister Alexander, popularly known as the Scissors. The Goths had found a new leader called Totila, an able general and politician, who promised to deliver the populace from Alexander and his henchmen. Totila also promised to free slaves and make a land distribution to all. In 543 CE, he retook Naples, and by the following year, he had retaken most of the cities that had fallen into Byzantine hands. Belisarius, with inadequate forces, was unable to stem the tide, and he was recalled to the east, where he was needed to combat a new threat from the Persians.

Justinian replaced Belisarius with the elderly eunuch **Narses**, who had proved his military capacities as commander of the palace guard. Narses arrived in Italy in 552 CE with a large army that included many Germanic contingents. Marching south, he encountered the forces of Totila at the Battle of Busta Gallorum. The Byzantine army, with its superior numbers, made short work of the opposition, and Totila was fatally wounded in the combat. Narses continued south to take Rome itself, and by 553 CE, the last pocket of Gothic resistance had finally been broken.

The Italy that Narses offered to his emperor was poverty stricken and exhausted. The land had been ravaged by constant warfare, many of the cities were in ruins, and famine and disease were rife. The population hated their new rulers and their exorbitant tax policies. Above all, Rome, the eternal city, had been totally destroyed. The water that flowed from its smashed aqueducts turned the surrounding countryside into an unhealthy swampland. The Circus Maximus was abandoned, and the famous baths would never function again. The beautiful marble statues that had once adorned the city squares had been broken up and used as projectiles against the Goths. The destruction was irreversible, and the city would remain in ruins throughout the Middle Ages.

Campaigning in Spain

Disruption within the Visigothic kingdom in Spain gave Justinian an opportunity to intervene there. In 550 CE, he began yet another campaign, landing an army in southeastern Spain. His troops succeeded in reconquering the coastal area, but they were unable to proceed farther inland because the Goths united against them, blocking the advance.

This limited success in Spain was Justinian's last conquest. Over the course of his long reign, he had managed to regain most of the lands on the perimeter of the Mediterranean that had once been part of the Roman Empire. Only Gaul and northern Spain remained outside his control. However, when he died in 565 CE, the empire's borders were already beginning to crumble.

Justinian's Legal Code

Justinian is not remembered only for his wars of conquest and his efforts to reunite the Roman Empire. One of his greatest achievements was the work he commissioned to codify the mass of edicts, precedents, and judicial decisions that made up the tangled Roman legal system. A commission of legal scholars, under the direction of the jurist Tribonian, worked for ten years to bring order to the enormous number of laws and the chaos of imperial jurisprudence. The result of their efforts was published under the title *Corpus Juris Civilis* (Body of Civil Law).

The code had three parts. The first part was a compilation of all the laws (since the reign of Hadrian) that were still valid. The second part, the *Digesta*, was a summary of the legal tracts of the great Roman legal scholars from the time of the emperors. The third part, the *Institutiones*, was an introduction to law for students. The entire document was approved by the legislative authority in 534 CE and was periodically updated by the inclusion of new decrees.

Like any code of jurisprudence, the *Corpus Juris Civilis* was a systematic compilation of previously existing statutes. Its influence

This manuscript page from the *Corpus Juris Civilis* dates to the fourteenth century CE. Justinian's legal code serves as the foundation for modern Western jurisprudence.

long outlived the empire, and it constituted the basis of civil law in much of the Western world, serving as the foundation for the laws of many European countries. A Spanish version became the basis of law in many South American countries.

Justinian's Legacy

Historians are divided about Justinian's political achievements. Some claim he was a great politician, while others call him a fanatic for trying to realize his dream of a world-encompassing empire. His constant wars left the empire on the brink of bankruptcy, and his critics claim that he failed to understand the mood of his time. The migration of the Germanic peoples could not be stemmed, nor could the impoverishment and depopulation of the western provinces be easily reversed. The financial cost of the armies and of the many new fortifications built along the frontiers could no longer be met, and Byzantine power began to crumble almost immediately after Justinian's death in 565 CE.

New enemies were already waiting in the wings. The Avers, a people related to the Huns, appeared in 568 CE in southern Russia and in the Balkans, driving the Lombards into Italy. At the same time, the Slavs crossed the Danube in great numbers. In the seventh century CE, the Arabs would begin their march of triumph in Asia and Africa, and the holdings of the Byzantine Empire would dwindle to not much more than Anatolia and a few bridgeheads in Europe.

This mosaic of Mary and the infant Jesus is from the Hagia Sophia. The role of Mary in Christian theology was hotly debated among early Christians and continues to be a source of disagreement for Christians today.

CHAPTER NINE

Early Christian Theology

While Christianity was becoming the dominant religion of the Roman Empire in the first four centuries CE, its beliefs were being developed and codified. This theology has remained at the heart of Christian teaching.

For their beliefs, many early Christians were punished with death, becoming martyrs, and martyrdom was a key element of Christian belief. Dying for one's faith was believed to wash away a victim's sins so that he or she immediately became a saint. Each saint had his or her special day of remembrance. Saints were believed to demonstrate their power through a wide range of miracles.

The first recognized martyr was Stephen, one of the original seven deacons of the early church in Jerusalem. In 36 CE, Stephen was charged, by the Jewish authorities, with blasphemy for preaching about Christ's message and resurrection and calling for changes in the Torah (the Jewish law). When Stephen was brought before the Sanhedrin (the Jewish council), he was condemned to death by stoning.

Stephen's death initiated an era of Christian persecution in Jerusalem. The city's small Christian sect fled, many of them taking refuge in Rome. After a great fire badly damaged Rome in 64 CE, however, the emperor Nero falsely accused the Christians of starting the fire, and many of them were put to death.

From that time on, Christians in the Roman Empire suffered occasional persecution. It reached a height under the emperor **Domitian**, who came to the throne in 81 CE and tried to eliminate

Christianity from his empire. Thousands of Christians were crucified, burned alive, or killed with swords. In the arena, they were torn to pieces by wild animals as a spectacle for the Roman masses.

Debating Mary's Status

theodosius iunior impersimoodus effes quecc sci patris cu imperatore conf cruire et subscripserunt;

Theodosius II presided over the debates at the Council of Ephesus.

Another key element of the early church was the cult of the Virgin Mary, the mother of Christ. Mary was revered as the Mother of God to emphasize the divinity of Christ. She was also a contrast to Eve, the first woman in the Bible. Eve had disobeyed God, while Mary had accepted her destiny and said to the Angel Gabriel, "Behold the handmaiden of the Lord." Saint Irenaeus, writing near the end of the second century CE, remarked: "The bonds in which Eve fettered us by her disobedience have been released by the obedience of Mary. What the virgin Eve bound by her fault has been freed by the Virgin Mary through her faith."

In the fourth century CE, the Syrian monk Nestorius maintained that Mary should not be called the Mother of God but the Mother of Christ. However, in 431 CE, a church council met at **Ephesus** (in modern-day Turkey) to debate questions of Christian doctrine. The council condemned Nestorius's view. In both the orthodox and Roman Catholic churches, Mary has been called the Mother of God ever since.

At around the time the cult of Mary began, angels also began to be venerated. Jewish scriptures had described angels as spirits or supernatural beings who served God. In the Christian church, angels came to occupy a crucial position as the messengers of God. They were divided into groups, including the seraphim and cherubim, and some had individual names. The archangel Michael, for example, was believed to have cast the evil angel Lucifer out of heaven. The fallen angel reigned over hell as Satan.

Christians believed that the souls of the saved found eternal happiness in heaven among the angels and saints. Heaven was assumed to be located somewhere above Earth. Hell, to which the souls of the damned were sent, was a place of eternal fire thought to be deep beneath the earth.

Baptism

The early church preached that believing in "Christian" values, such as faith, hope, and love, would not alone earn salvation; believers also had to undergo baptism. Ritual cleansing by immersion in water had a long history. It was practiced under Jewish law and had been part of the mystery cults of ancient Greece. The Bible told the story of how John the Baptist had baptized Christ himself. By the second century CE, the baptism of converts was widespread, usually accompanied by the words, "I baptize you in the name of the Father, and of the Son, and of the Holy Spirit."

This third-century CE fresco depicts a Christian baptism scene. It was found in the Catacombs of San Callisto in Rome, Italy.

Adopting a Jewish idea that young children were part of the religious community, early Christians probably baptized infants as soon as they were born. In the case of young children, the ritual took the form of sprinkling with water, rather than total immersion. Not all converts were baptized immediately. The Roman emperor Constantine did not receive the sacrament until he was on his deathbed. Saint Augustine, one of the fathers of the church, is thought to have regretted that he was baptized so late.

The second-century CE Christian theologian Tertullian left a description of the baptism ritual for adults as it was performed in Carthage. The candidates for baptism made a formal declaration that they renounced the devil and his works. They were then immersed in a pool three times, to symbolize that they had been born again. After taking a sip of milk and honey, they were anointed with oil, and a priest laid his hands on them to instill the Holy Spirit. Once baptized, the initiates could then participate in other Christian rituals.

Communion with God

The central rite of Christianity is the **Eucharist** (communion), which marks the remembrance of the last supper that Christ shared with his disciples. The Eucharist involves the sharing of bread and wine that have been *consecrated* (blessed). Christians believe that the ritual follows the command Christ made as he gave bread and wine to his disciples: "Do this in remembrance of me." By the second century CE, specific rules for the Eucharist had been laid down in the *Didache*, one of the earliest texts to specify rules for Christian ritual: "Every Sunday, gather together to break bread and give thanks, after you have confessed your sins, so that your sacrifice is pure." The second-century CE Saint Justin described the ritual in more detail. He listed twelve steps, including the consecration of the bread and wine, when (some people believed) the items became the actual body and blood of Christ.

Disagreements continue today about the nature of the Eucharist. Is it a mystical sacrament, in which bread and wine become the body and blood of Christ? Or is it merely a ritual practiced in remembrance? Certainly, the practice varied in different parts of the Roman Empire. By the fourth century CE, there were four major variants of the Eucharist, named after Antioch, Alexandria, Rome, and Gaul.

The Christian sacrament of communion dates back to the Last Supper between Jesus and his disciples.

The Church and Sinners

Considerable debate went on among the leaders of the early church as to what its attitude should be toward sinners, given that sin was accepted as being inevitable. Christ had told the apostles to forgive people their sins, but there was much controversy over exactly how far the instruction should be taken. Tertullian, for example, advocated a very severe attitude toward sinners. Writing around 200 CE, he argued that forgiveness could only be obtained through baptism. Any sins committed after baptism were unforgivable.

In 220 CE, Pope Callixus expressed a milder attitude. Sins should be forgiven as often as necessary, he said, so long as the sinner was repentant and determined not to sin again. Repentance had to be expressed openly, and sinners had to do penance, such as being excluded from the community of the faithful for a period of time. In serious cases, such a banishment (**excommunication**) could last an entire lifetime. However, even in this case, the possibility of ultimate forgiveness was not denied; a sinner could repent on his or her death bed and receive the last rites of forgiveness.

Understanding Manichaeism

Manichaeism was a popular philosophy from Persia, where it was founded in the third century CE by **Mani**, who regarded himself as the final prophet in a line that included Zoroaster, Buddha, and Christ. Supporters of Manichaeism claimed that it was the true form of Christianity, but many Christians regarded it as heresy.

The philosophy maintained that the world was divided into opposites: good and evil, light and dark. The human soul is entangled with evil and can only be freed by living a life of abstinence from both material desires and desires of the flesh. At death, the soul of a person who has led a righteous life may enter paradise. The souls of those who have succumbed to the pleasures of the flesh are stuck on Earth and condemned to a cycle of rebirth.

The Life of Saint Augustine

One of the most important theologians of the early church was Augustine. He was born in 354 CE in the small town of Tagaste (present-day Souk-Ahras) in the Roman province of Numidia (in what is now Algeria). Augustine's father, Patricius, adhered to a pagan religion, but his mother, Monica, was a devout Christian. The young Augustine showed such promise that his parents sent him to study rhetoric in Carthage, the most important city in northern Africa, hoping that he would eventually get a post in the civil service. In Carthage, Augustine began a relationship with a woman who bore him a son in 372 CE. He named the boy *Adeodatus*, Latin for "gift from God."

In Carthage, Augustine discovered an essay by the first-century BCE Roman statesman Cicero. The essay, entitled "Hortensius," argued that people can only achieve happiness by leading a moral, contemplative life in the pursuit of truth. Inspired to seek out his own philosophy, Augustine adopted Manichaeism in 373 CE. Nine years later, he abandoned Manichaeism in favor of Skepticism, the Greek doctrine that all knowledge is open to question.

In 383 CE, Augustine sailed for Rome. There, he came to the attention of the pagan senator Symmachus, who had tried to convince the Christian emperor Valentinian II to restore a statue of Victory that had been removed from the senate. Symmachus was instrumental in setting Augustine up as a teacher of rhetoric in Milan.

Augustine eventually became interested in **Neoplatonism** (see sidebar, page 124), which taught that there was a transcendental Good to which everyone should aspire. He also remained interested in Christianity, however. In a famous autobiographical work entitled *Confessions*, Augustine recorded how, while meditating, he had experienced a mystical "changeless light," which he interpreted as an experience of God. On a later occasion, he was walking in a garden when he heard a voice saying, "Take and read." Augustine opened the New Testament at Paul's Epistle to the Romans, and the sentence he read made it clear to him that he was intended to convert to Christianity. He and his son were baptized on Easter Eve, 387 CE, by Bishop Ambrose of Milan.

Augustine returned to Tagaste, where he set up a small community with a group of friends to devote his life to the contemplation of religious subjects. He was ordained as a priest in 391 CE and became assistant to the bishop of Hippo. Augustine continued to write and became a prominent local orator. When the bishop died, Augustine took his place in 396 CE and was bishop until his own death in 430 CE.

Unlike many of his colleagues, Augustine was not ambitious for advancement. In his cloister, he could pursue his intellectual activities unhindered. He dictated at great speed to an *amanuensis* (secretary), sending a steady stream of publications throughout the empire.

The church at that time was split by heresy; variations of Christian belief existed side by side, all claiming to be the true faith. Augustine launched fierce attacks on heresy and laid out his own definitions of the freedom of human beings and how they could achieve salvation. Augustine's first attacks condemned the Manichaeans, to whose philosophy he had once subscribed.

Augustine rejected the Manichaean view that the world was forever in conflict between good and evil. He argued that the world was created by God and, therefore, must be good. Augustine also rejected the Manichaean argument that only the "elect" (who led righteous lives) would attain heaven after death and that the "auditors" (people who served the elect) could only hope for rebirth on Earth. He insisted that humans had free will and could attain salvation through divine grace. In addition, he rejected the Manichaean belief in the transmigration of souls (the passing of a soul to another body after death) because he believed that every soul was unique.

Mystical Neoplatonism

Neoplatonism was a development of the teachings of Plato, the Greek philosopher of the fifth century BCE. Its founder was Plotinus, who studied philosophy in Alexandria in the early part of the third century CE and later traveled in Asia before settling in Rome. There he taught his own brand of Platonism, which maintained that there is a hierarchy of being, the highest level of which is the supreme principle, which may be called the One or the Good. This ultimate reality cannot be known by the mind, and humans can only aspire to reach it by looking inward to themselves. Neoplatonism is a form of mysticism.

The Donatists

One of the heresies Augustine was called upon to refute was that of the **Donatists,** a powerful sect in the African church. The Donatists argued that the Christian sacrament had to be administered by a priest who was without sin because a priest who had sinned would be unable to convey the Holy Spirit to communicants. Augustine believed that no man was without sin and argued that the condition of the priest was irrelevant. The Holy Spirit was conveyed to communicants by the power of Christ alone, not by whoever happened to administer the sacrament.

The *Confessions*

Augustine's *Confessions*, written between 397 and 401 CE, is one of the few personal writings in ancient literature. In thirteen books, he described his life up through his conversion to Christianity at age thirty-three. The first ten books deal with his pagan youth, in which he describes his own desires and weaknesses with great frankness. He was long attracted to Christianity. However, he was put off by the church's condemnation of worldly pleasures.

This painting of St. Augustine was made in the fifteenth century CE.

Augustine described his inner turmoil before his conversion: "I suffered and tormented myself and turned about in the chains that still held me with a weak shackle, which nevertheless kept me in bondage. I said to myself: Onward! Delay no longer! I resolved to begin and did nothing."

"This internal struggle," he continued, "was a duel with myself. I ran back into the garden and gave free rein to my tears, crying out: How long, oh Lord? How long?" Instinctively, Augustine must have known that the moment of his conversion was near. "I spoke and wept with all the bitterness of a broken heart. And suddenly, I heard from an adjacent house a child's voice, or the voice of a young girl, that was singing and repeating these words: Take and read, take and read. It occurred to me that the words could be the refrain in a child's game, though I could not remember anything of the sort. I went back to the place where I had been sitting earlier and where I had left the book with the epistles of Paul. I picked it up and opened it, and my eyes fell on the following words: You shall not live in excess and debauchery, but follow Jesus Christ. I had scarcely finished reading the line when something like a light spread through my heart and dispelled the darkness of my uncertainty."

Adam, Eve, and Original Sin

Another great controversy within the church was that of original sin, the sin committed when Adam disobeyed God in the Garden of Eden. The accepted church teaching was that everyone inherited the guilt of Adam's sin at birth; it could only be removed by baptism into the church. However, Augustine's contemporary, the British monk Pelagius, denied the concept of original sin. Pelagius argued that people were born without sin and that, if a baby died, it would go to heaven whether or not it was baptized. The African bishops condemned Pelagius's views and accused him of nine principal errors, including the ideas that Adam died simply because he was mortal and not as a punishment for his inherent sin and that Adam alone, rather than the whole of humankind, was punished for his sin.

Augustine, in his efforts to counter Pelagius's views, was forced to define his own views on divine sovereignty, original sin, and predestination. The key issue, as he saw it, was whether or not all souls had become sinful through Adam's fall. Based on his reading of the Bible, Augustine concluded that they had. The soul could be cleansed of sin, he reasoned, but only by the grace of God. This was the opposite of the conclusion Pelagius had reached. According to the British monk, God had given people reason and freedom to choose for themselves whether to be saved or damned. Salvation depended on the will of each individual to live without sin.

Augustine's response was to articulate the concept of predestination. Even before birth, he argued, people were predestined to go to either heaven or hell. He pointed to his own life, which had shown him how futile it was to try to earn salvation. For twenty years, he had explored spirituality and belief, yet he had only found salvation after an experience of God. Moreover, he insisted that God knew what people's lives held in store. How God's plan interacted with human freedom of will, he admitted, was beyond the grasp of human understanding.

Augustine's Writings

Augustine wrote many works, including the autobiographical *Confessions*. Between 413 and 426 CE, he wrote the twenty-two books that make up his *De Civitate Dei* (*The City of God*), a defense of Christianity in the face of a pagan belief that the new religion was responsible for the downfall of the Roman Empire. The belief was especially common after the Visigoths sacked Rome in 410 CE.

In the first ten books of *De Civitate Dei*, Augustine attacked pagan religion; he then traced the history and development of the Christian church in another twelve volumes. Explaining why he felt Christianity should take the place of paganism, he expounded the Christian view of the great struggle between good and evil. History, he wrote, was moving slowly toward the climax of the Last Judgment, when the citizens of the City of God would be saved and the rest damned.

Augustine also wrote hundreds of letters, 270 of which appear in his *Epistles*, written between 386 and 429 CE. He also wrote commentaries on the Bible and many treatises on religious subjects.

Augustine died in Hippo in 430 CE, when Vandals were besieging the city. Although the Roman state he had lived in was dying, his work was not lost.

This seventeenth century painting by Francisco Collantes depicts St. Paul of Thebes, Christianity's first hermit.

CHAPTER TEN

The First Monastics

Between the second and the sixth centuries CE, a number of influential Christian thinkers opted to abandon conventional society and adopt a life of seclusion. Among the most famous was Saint Benedict, who established a monastery at Monte Cassino.

The urge to withdraw from society and follow a life of contemplation and prayer is common to many religions. From the early history of Christianity, seclusion and monasticism, or living in a monastery (see sidebar, page 135), appealed to many believers.

The First Hermit: Saint Paul of Thebes

The first Christian hermit is generally considered to be **Paul of Thebes** (ca. 230–341 CE). Paul was a wealthy Egyptian who had embraced the Christian faith. He fled into the desert to escape persecution under the Roman emperor Decius. Remaining in the desert even after the emperor died, Paul lived in poverty in a cave where he followed a regime of prayer and self-denial. He is reputed to have lived to a great age and to have been visited by Saint **Anthony** of Egypt (himself sometimes cited as the first Christian hermit) when Paul was 113 years old. It was said that the two hermits had such a lengthy conversation that God sent a raven to bring them bread for a meal.

Saint Anthony of Egypt

Saint Anthony, who lived from around 251 to 356 CE, followed the example of Paul of Thebes. He gave away his considerable wealth and withdrew from the world to live a life of deliberate hardship, first in an unused rock tomb cut into a mountain overlooking the Nile River and then in the ruins of an Egyptian fortress. Finding even this accommodation too luxurious to fit with his idea of a spiritual life, he quit the fortress to travel the barren, windy desert between the Nile River and the Red Sea. During twenty years of solitude, Anthony was repeatedly assailed by visions of the devil presenting him with temptations. He resisted the attacks with prayer and acts of penitence.

In spite of his desire for solitude, Anthony was joined in the desert by other Christians fleeing Roman persecution. Around 311 CE, Anthony abandoned his hermit's life and helped to organize a community of Christians who sought personal solitude within a monastic life. Anthony established guidelines for life within the community and is therefore regarded as the father of Christian monasticism.

Anthony died at the age of 104, and his life was written by Saint Athanasius, the bishop of Alexandria and a friend of Anthony. Athanasius's work was the first hagiography (biography of a saint), and its lively style evoked a vivid picture of a hermit who remained deeply interested in the world he had given up. "What are the people up to?" Athanasius records him asking visitors. "Do cities still exist? Who rules the earth, and do people still fall prey to the devil?"

The Appeal of Monasticism

The motives that led people to adopt a monastic life or the life of a hermit were complex. Some Christians became ascetics (people who live a life of self-denial) because they believed it brought them closer to God. Others focused on the fight against the temptations of the flesh, which they believed came from the devil. As Christianity spread, pagan idols and temples began to disappear. Many Christians believed that the pagan gods were demons who took refuge in the desert when their former dwelling places were destroyed. In order to fight these demons, or the devil himself, a pious Christian in Egypt, Syria, or Palestine could seek them out in the wilderness.

Exploring the Life of Saint Anthony

Much of what is known about Saint Anthony comes from a long account written in the fourth century CE by Bishop Athanasius of Alexandria. Athanasius's account was the first hagiography (biography of a saint) and set the form for the literary genre, which became very popular among Christians in the Middle Ages.

Athanasius sketches Anthony's character and then tells how, at age twenty, the wealthy young man is so impressed by Christian teaching that he gives away his inheritance and becomes a hermit. When temptations come from Satan, Anthony resists them, leaving his village and taking up residence in an empty tomb. The devil tries to seduce him with obscene images but only evokes greater purity in the hermit, who justifies his way of life by saying: "Like the fish which dies out of water, the hermit dies out of the desert."

Anthony moves deeper into the desert. People flock to him for advice or abandon their homes to join him. Anthony, obeying a divine voice, moves deeper into the desert. When disciples descend on him again, he organizes them into a loose community. In the final section of the work, God notifies Anthony of the time of his death, and the saint prepares himself and leaves instructions for his burial.

The almost complete lack of hard facts and chronological data became characteristic of hagiography, as did tales of a saint's visions and mysterious knowledge, such as Anthony's ability to read the thoughts of the people who come to him and to foresee his own death. This serves to prove that he is a saint, as do the witnesses to Anthony's miracles. Anthony attains increasingly saintly qualities, until he can finally vanquish Satan.

Later hagiographies follow a similar pattern. The saint becomes removed from mortal life to gain heavenly status. The saint is also distinguished by a type of modesty. He or she claims to perform miracles or utter prophecies only through the power of God. It is not the saint who has the power, but God. As Anthony himself warned, "Do not rejoice when the spirits obey you, but that your name shall be written in heaven."

Toward the end of the third century CE, many Christians adopted an ascetic life. Some chose solitude, living as hermits. Others, particularly in Egypt and western Asia, sought life in a community dedicated to the worship of God.

Organized Monasticism

Pachomius (ca. 290–346 CE) was an Egyptian soldier who converted to Christianity while he was serving in the army of the emperor Constantine. On quitting the army, Pachomius became a disciple of Saint Anthony in the desert. Later, Pachomius established the first proper monastery on an island already used by hermits in the Nile River. He built an enclosure to surround the hermits' scattered cells. He also drew up rules for the hermits to follow; they were the first set of *cenobitic* (monastic) rules laid down. The rules divided the day into set periods of prayer and labor and placed the monks under the authority of an abbot, who ensured that they followed the rules.

The main purpose of Pachomius's rules was to give each individual the best possible opportunity to achieve his own spiritual purification (the first monks were all male). The concept of service to others, which was a feature of later monasteries, was largely absent. Aspiring monks had to wait seven days in front of the monastery's gate before they were admitted. Once accepted, they undertook a *novitiate* (trial period) of three years. When they were fully admitted to the community, they lived a life completely detached from the outside world.

The monks were required to take a vow of celibacy and had to bind themselves to obey the monastic rule, which included silence at all times. They lived three to a cell and ate meals communally, with their heads covered. Only in rigidly prescribed circumstances were they allowed to express themselves through gestures. The community supported itself through agriculture, raising livestock, and weaving mats and baskets for sale. The division of labor was organized by the abbot.

In spite of the strictness of his rules, Pachomius attracted thousands of followers. He founded nine more similar communities (including one for women, which was supervised by his sister) before his death in 346 CE. A century later, an estimated fifty thousand monks lived in Pachomian monasteries.

Saint Basil and Eastern Monasticism

In spite of the success of Pachomius in Egypt, Basil of Caesarea is generally recognized as the patriarch of eastern monasticism. Basil was born to a wealthy Christian family in 329 CE in Caesarea Mazaca (present-day Kayseri in Turkey) near the Black Sea. As a young man, he was sent to Constantinople and Athens to train as a lawyer and orator. Following his studies, Basil toured Palestine and Egypt, where he became acquainted with the desert monks, who at that time were attracting much academic interest.

Basil was impressed by the ascetic way of life. Around 360 CE, he set up his own monastic community on his family's estate at Annesi. He made a study of various forms of monasticism, which he divided into four categories: desert hermits, ascetics who lived together in unorganized communities, wandering holy men, and monks living in organized monasteries. Basil rejected the solitary life of the hermit in favor of monasticism, reasoning that a community of spiritually oriented people should aim to achieve the ideal of brotherly love. "The solitary life has only one goal," he wrote, "the service of its own interests. That is clearly opposed to the law of love."

Basil was not able to enjoy his monastic life for long; he was called away by the church for important assignments, principally to defend it against the heresy of Arianism. Before he left Annesi, however, Basil drew up a detailed monastic rule that is still used by some Roman Catholic orders and most orthodox monasteries. Basil's strictures were divided into the Longer Rules, with fifty-three questions and answers, and the Shorter Rules, which provided solutions to more than three hundred problems that might arise in a monk's life.

Basil believed that the ascetic life was the purest form of Christianity. Because monks were the true believers, they were obliged to imitate the example of Christ and the apostles down to the smallest detail. To discover these details, Basil said, the abbot would give the most able monks the opportunity to study the scriptures. The scholarly monks would form a board of advisors to the abbot and would hear any complaints from individual monks about their treatment. Obedience to the abbot was compulsory. Any dissent was treated like a disease. The dissenter was sent to the hospital ward to recover, and if he did

St. Basil (*standing, left*) instituted a famous monastic code that sought to imitate the lifestyle of Jesus Christ and the apostles.

not abandon resistance to the abbot, he was ejected from the community, in accordance with Basil's belief that "insubordination and distrust are the result of a number of sins, doubtful faith, pride, and misbehavior."

The monks were required to meet in prayer eight times a day, and Basil described the meetings in mystical and poetic terms. Prayer did not release the monks from the duty of labor. "He who wants to eat must work," Basil insisted. Absolute poverty among the monks was not required, however. Monks were allowed to have personal possessions and to live in individual rather than shared cells. Basil saw this as allowing each monk to achieve his greatest spiritual potential in his own way, but in practice, the freedom fostered abuse.

In addition to his famous monastic rule, Basil wrote three books opposing the theories of the Arian theologian Eunomius, collectively entitled *Against Eunomius*. His other works included a treatise entitled *On the Holy Spirit and Moralia,* a collection of verses from the New Testament.

Basil was ordained as a priest and became assistant to the bishop of Caesarea. Several years later, on the death of the bishop in 370 CE, Basil was himself elected to the position. He held the post until his death in January of 379 CE and was made a saint soon after.

Three generations of Basil's family are venerated as saints, including his grandmother Macrina; his parents, Basil and Emmelia; his sister Macrina; and his brothers Peter of Sebaste and Gregory of Nyssa. Basil, Gregory, and their friend Gregory of Nazianzus are called the Cappadocian Fathers.

Saint Simeon and the Stylites

Simeon Stylites was a fifth-century CE ascetic who sought solitude on top of a pillar. His example was imitated by later ascetics who were known as stylites; *stylos* is a Greek word meaning "pillar."

Simeon was born in Syria around 390 CE. After starting life as a shepherd, he entered a monastery. Simeon practiced mortification (causing himself physical pain or discomfort in order to bring himself closer to God). He buried himself up to the chin for months on end and later bound his waist until the skin rotted. These measures proved too extreme for Simeon's abbot, who expelled him from the community.

Simeon became a hermit, but the stories of the miracles he had performed brought many visitors to his hermitage. Around 422 CE, in order to escape the visitors, Simeon climbed to the top of a pillar that

Understanding Monasticism

The word *monasticism* derives from the Greek word *monos*, meaning "alone." It is used to describe the life of religious people who choose to withdraw from the world to worship God, either alone, as a hermit, or in a community of monks or nuns. Monasticism always involves a life of self-denial. The hermit or monk embraces poverty and celibacy and, in some cases, will choose to remain silent and to mortify his or her own flesh by wearing a hair shirt or by flagellation. He or she may also fast regularly and spend much time in prayer and contemplation.
A community of monks living in a monastery may elect to engage with their local community. In the past, monks were often self-supporting, farming their land and breeding fish in ponds.
Some monks held church services that were open to villagers. Monasteries also offered accommodation for travelers and medical care for the sick. The monastery libraries were also important repositories of knowledge. Some monks were constantly occupied in copying old manuscripts or compiling histories.

was 60 feet (20m) tall and remained day and night on a small platform surrounded by a railing to stop him from falling off. Simeon stayed on the pillar for thirty-seven years, with no protection from the elements and no food or water apart from what was brought up to him by ladder. He spent most of his time praying, but twice a day, he preached to the many pilgrims who congregated around the base of the pillar.

Simeon died in 459 CE, but his influence lasted for seven centuries. Others who followed his example included his disciple Saint Daniel, who lived from 409 to 493 CE, and the seventh-century CE saint Alypius, who reputedly stayed on top of his pillar for sixty-seven years.

Western Monastics

Monasticism was brought to the west by Bishop Athanasius of Alexandria. Athanasius (ca. 293–373) spent most of his life supporting the orthodox view that Christ was of the same substance as God the Father. That put Athanasius at odds with the Arian heresy (which held that Christ was of a different substance) and the emperors who supported the Arian view. Athanasius was repeatedly exiled from Egypt. When banishment took him to Rome, he introduced the concept of the monastic life to Italy. He also wrote *The Life of Saint Anthony*, which was instrumental in popularizing the idea of the ascetic and monastic life among Christians. In northern Africa, Augustine, bishop of Hippo from 396 to 430 CE, was responsible for introducing the ideal of the monastic life. It was introduced to Gaul (present-day France) by Saint **Martin of Tours**.

Martin of Tours (ca. 316–397 CE) was born in Sabaria in Pannonia (present-day Szombathely in Hungary), where his father, a Roman soldier, was stationed. Martin converted to Christianity at age ten and later served in the Roman army. After the army, he lived as a hermit for a while, before making his way to Poitiers in Gaul. He became a disciple of Hilary, the bishop of Poitiers, and joined in his fight against Arianism. After traveling as a missionary in Pannonia, Illyricum, and Italy, Martin returned to found Gaul's first monastery at Ligugé.

In 371 CE, Martin was appointed bishop of Tours, a post he accepted with reluctance. To enable him to retreat to the monastic life whenever possible, he founded the monastery at Marmoutier just outside Tours. Marmoutier became a monastic center from which missionaries spread Christianity to Celtic peoples throughout Gaul. Martin's biography was written by Sulpicius Severus, who attributed a number of miracles to his friend. Sulpicius also described an incident in which Martin met a beggar on a freezing winter's day and cut his own cloak in half in order to cover the shivering man. That night, Christ, wearing the monk's cloak, appeared to Martin in a dream and thanked him for his generosity to the beggar.

In the early fifth century CE, monasticism in Gaul received a further boost when John Cassian founded the Abbey of Saint-Victor at Marseille. Cassian (360–435 CE), who became an influential theologian, lived for fifteen years as a desert hermit in Egypt before becoming a priest. Around 415 CE, he traveled to Marseille, where he founded a nunnery as well as the Saint-Victor monastery, of which he himself became abbot. For the next twenty years, Cassian devoted himself to writing theological works, of which Institutes of *the Monastic Life and Conferences of the Egyptian Monks* were to have a great influence on the development of monasticism in the west. The *Institutes* sets out the structures necessary for a monastic life, while the *Conferences* discusses the nature of spirituality. The works earned Cassian the title by which he is commonly known: the Lawgiver of Monastic Life.

Saint Jerome and the Vulgate

Another early monk who was to play a decisive role in the history of Christianity in the west was Saint **Jerome** (ca. 345–420 CE). He was born to Christian parents in Stridon, Dalmatia, and around age twelve was sent to Rome to study. Jerome became familiar with both pagan and Christian literature and fluent in Latin, Greek, and Hebrew. Around age twenty, Jerome embarked on a period of travel, living as an ascetic in the desert and continuing to study the scriptures. He became attracted by the monastic life. Although Jerome was ordained a priest in 379 CE, he accepted ordination only on condition that it should not interfere with his aspirations to become a monk.

This painting by Caravaggio depicts St. Jerome, who translated the original Greek bible into Latin.

Jerome spent the next three years in Constantinople with the theologian Gregory of Nazianzus to continue his study of the scriptures. Then, in 382 CE, Jerome returned to Rome, where he was made secretary to Pope Damasus I. Jerome made attempts to popularize the idea of the ascetic life, teaching classes on the monastic ideal to aristocratic Romans. Two of Jerome's students, the wealthy widow Paula (later Saint Paula) and her daughter, Eustochium, followed him to Bethlehem after the death of Damasus in 385 CE. There, they founded a convent for women and a monastery for men, of which Jerome became abbot.

Jerome lived at the monastery in Bethlehem for the rest of his life and produced an enormous number of theological works, many of which were commentaries on the Bible or rebuttals of heresies. Jerome's major work was the translation of the Bible from Greek and Hebrew into Latin. Jerome's version of the Bible (known as the Vulgate) was used by the Roman Catholic Church for centuries.

Benedict of Nursia

The undisputed father of monasticism in the west was **Benedict of Nursia** (ca. 480–547 CE), founder of the order of Beneditine monks. Benedict was born to a prominent family in Nursia, Italy, and was later sent to study in Rome. He found the city so degenerate, however, that he retreated to live in a cave near Subiaco, around 40 miles (64 km) to the east. He stayed in the cave for three years. During that time, he was fed by a monk from a nearby monastery and was visited by crowds of disciples, who were drawn by his growing reputation for saintliness. Benedict accepted an invitation to become abbot of one of the monasteries in the area, but his efforts to introduce reforms provoked jealousies among the monks. Learning of a plot to poison him, Benedict abandoned his position. Later, in 529 CE, Benedict established a monastery at Monte Cassino, between Rome and Naples. He lived there for the rest of his life, perfecting the set of rules that were to become the guiding light of all monastic institutions in the west for the next 1,500 years.

The rule of Saint Benedict stressed the importance of, among other things, communal living, communal property, physical labor, and the avoidance of unnecessary speech. New monks were required to spend one year on probation, and after that probationary period, they had to take a solemn oath of obedience to the rule and to the abbot.

The rule also offered words of advice to the abbot himself: "He who remembers that the word abbot means 'father' and proves this through his actions shall be worthy of ruling a monastery. He must be just, righteous, strict, and competent. He must be able to teach God's commandments with the aid of the Holy Scriptures. Through his example he shall guide those less studied to the way of the Lord."

The abbot had absolute power. Although he was supposed to consult the monks on certain matters, "he, after hearing the views of his brethren, must decide as he deems fit … All monks must be called because sometimes the Lord reveals himself to the youngest, which is the most suitable for the community." A meeting of the community was also responsible for electing a new abbot. "In the event the meeting elects an incompetent abbot, the bishop of the diocese where the monastery is located or the abbots of neighboring monasteries shall appoint an overseer worthy of ruling the house of God."

Regarding the way of life best suited to lead to the kingdom of God, Benedict's recommendation was short and clear: *ora et labora* (prayer and work). A monk should have around eight hours of sleep a night, with his waking hours divided more or less equally between prayer, manual labor, and study of the scriptures. The ordering of the daily services was laid down precisely, even to the kind of chants the monks used. They had to sing simple melodies in unison (later known as Gregorian chant), rather than singing different parts with harmonies.

Benedict forbade all personal property, and the monks had to sleep in large dormitories rather than single cells. Their food consisted of two light dishes a day, and meat was allowed only for the sick and the weak. Rather reluctantly, Benedict granted his monks half a pint (a quarter of a liter) of wine per day. "But those who abstain," he added, "shall reap their reward."

The aim of the monastery was to be self-sufficient. Therefore, farming was rated more valuable than intellectual and artistic pursuits. However, if any artists joined the monastery, Benedict noted, "they may be allowed to continue their work if they do so humbly." The artworks could be sold for the benefit of the monastery, but their prices were supposed to be lower than that of artworks produced by secular artists outside the monastery "so that God may be glorified in them, as in all things."

The Benedictine monks were industrious and broad-minded in their studies. Benedict permitted his monasteries to include the ancient Greek and Roman literature places in their libraries, even those works written by pagans. "All reasonable men will agree," he said, "that knowledge of all matters within our reach is the most important. And here I do not mean the knowledge that is loftier, such as ours (that is, the knowledge of God) but I mean external knowledge which many Christians despise as being perfidious, harmful, and likely to move us away from God … Those who argue his way are blind and unknowing, and want the entire world to resemble them so as to hide their personal shortcomings in the mass of people." Without Saint Benedict's enlightened attitude toward knowledge, which was also shared by some of his contemporaries, much of the literature produced by the ancient world might have been lost forever.

St. Benedict founded the Benedictine order of monks. Their motto, *ora et labora* (prayer and work), demanded discipline in every facet of their monastic life.

CHRONOLOGY

ca. 700 BCE
City of Byzantium founded.

190 BCE
Seleucid emperor Antiochus III defeated by Roman force at Magnesia ad Sipylum.

146 BCE
Carthage destroyed by Roman army; Carthaginian territory becomes Roman province of Africa.

63 BCE
Pompey the Great extends eastern frontier by annexing Syria.

30 BCE
Roman emperor Augustus annexes Egypt.

9 CE
Roman army destroyed at Battle of Teutoburg Forest; defeat brings end to Roman involvement in northern Germany.

36 CE
Stephen becomes first recognized Christian martyr.

64 CE
Persecution of Christians begins after Nero blames them for great fire in Rome.

117 CE
Roman Empire reaches greatest extent under Trajan.

ca. 122 CE
Construction of Hadrian's Wall begins in northern Britain.

180 CE
Commodus becomes Roman emperor on death of father, Marcus Aurelius.

196 CE
Roman emperor Septimius Severus razes Byzantium.

197 CE
Septimius Severus proves victorious after "sale" of title of emperor leads to civil war.

211 CE
Severus dies on campaign in Britain; son Caracalla succeeds him.

ca. 230 CE
Paul of Thebes born.

235 CE
Severus Alexander killed in riot; Severan dynasty ends.

251 CE
Goths cross Danube and defeat Decius.

259 CE
Legions in Gaul elect
Marcus Postumus emperor;
Gallic Empire established.

272 CE
Roman emperor Aurelian defeats
Queen Zenobia's Palmyran forces
and reclaims eastern provinces.

275 CE
Aurelian dies; replaced by Tacitus.

284 CE
Diocletian seizes power in
Rome; later divides empire
into four sections for
administrative purposes.

303 CE
Diocletian publishes anti-
Christian edict; widespread
persecution ensues.

312 CE
Constantine becomes western
emperor; converts to Christianity
around this time.

313 CE
Constantine and Licinius issue
Edict of Milan, protecting
Christian rights of worship.

324 CE
Constantine becomes sole
ruler of Roman Empire; makes
Byzantium his capital city.

325 CE
Council of Nicaea condemns
Arianism as heresy.

329 CE
Basil of Caesarea born.

330 CE
Byzantium becomes official
capital of Roman Empire and is
renamed Constantinople.

337 CE
Death of Constantine
prompts civil war.

354 CE
Augustine born in Tagaste.

ca. 360 CE
Basil of Caesarea sets up
monastery on family estate
at Annesi.

361 CE
Julian the Apostate becomes
emperor; attempts to reestablish
old Roman religion.

368 CE
Work completed on
Valens Aqueduct.

378 CE
Goths overwhelmingly defeat
Valens at Battle of Adrianople.

379 CE
Theodosius becomes Roman emperor and begins clampdown on old pagan practices.

381 CE
Second Ecumenical Council, held in Constantinople, reaffirms Nicene Creed.

387 CE
Augustine baptized in Milan.

ca. 390 CE
Simeon Stylites born in Syria.

394 CE
Theodosius reunites western and eastern empires.

395 CE
Roman Empire splits permanently on death of Theodosius I.

396 CE
Augustine becomes bishop of Hippo.

397 CE
Augustine starts to write autobiographical Confessions.

402 CE
Visigoths invade Italy. Roman garrison withdraws from Britain, leaving the country exposed to raids by Picts.

410 CE
Visigothic king Alaric sacks Rome.

413 CE
Augustine begins writing twenty-two books of *De civitate Dei* (*The City of God*).

415 CE
John Cassian founds Abbey of Saint-Victor in Marseille.

430 CE
Augustine dies.

431 CE
Council of Ephesus confirms Mary's status as Mother of God.

439 CE
Vandals capture Carthage.

450 CE
Marcian becomes eastern emperor on death of Theodosius II.

476 CE
Romulus Augustulus deposed by Odoacer; event marks end of western Roman Empire.

ca. 480 CE
Roman scholar Boethius born. Benedict born in Nursia, Italy.

488 CE
Emperor Zeno persuades Ostrogoths to move to northern Italy.

512 CE
Anastasius I puts down
Monophysitic revolt.

527 CE
Justinian becomes eastern
Roman emperor.

529 CE
Benedict founds Abbey of
Monte Cassino.

532 CE
Nika Revolt suppressed.

534 CE
Justinian's legal code approved.

537 CE
Hagia Sophia inaugurated in
Constantinople.

565 CE
Justinian dies.

GLOSSARY

Alans Originally a Persian steppe people who settled in Scythia in the fourth century BCE. Conquered by the Huns, they later became allies.

Alemanni Southern Germanic people; threatened Roman borders and invaded Gaul in the third century CE; conquered eastern Gaul in the fourth century CE; defeated by the Frankish king Clovis I.

Aquitania Area of Gaul between the Pyrenees and the Garonne River.

Arianism Doctrine of fourth-century CE theologian Arius; held that Jesus Christ was not of the same substance as God, but merely the greatest of created beings.

Bactrians People from the ancient country of Bactria, which lay between the mountains of the Hindu Kush and the Amu Darya (ancient Oxus River) in what is now part of Afghanistan, Uzbekistan, and Tajikistan.

Blues Political party in Constantinople that organized important horse races against the Greens. Despite the lack of a clear political program, they had great influence on politics and religion.

Byzantium Ancient Greek city on the shore of the Bosporus; later known as Constantinople; modern Istanbul.

Carpi Ancient Dacian people who inhabited the Carpathian Mountains in modern Romania.

Celts Name given to a group of people occupying central and western Europe (from the British Isles to Hungary) by 1000 BCE. Bearers of the Celtic civilization are the Hallstatt and La Tène cultures; the Urnfield culture also has Celtic characteristics.

Constantinople Name for Byzantium (present-day Istanbul), which became the (Christian) residence of the emperor Constantine in 330 CE. In 395 CE, it became the capital of the eastern Roman Empire.

Ctesiphon Capital of the ancient Persian Empire.

Dacia Area of the Carpathian Mountains and Transylvania, in present-day Romania.

Demeter Greek goddess of the earth and agriculture.

Donatists Northern African Christians who believed that the holy sacraments could be administered only by priests who were without sin; named for their leader, Donatus (died ca. 355 CE); denounced by Augustine; outlawed as heretics.

Eboracum Roman name for the modern city of York, England.

Eleusinian Mysteries Secret religious rites in ancient Greece that involved the worship of the earth goddess Demeter.

Ephesus, Council of Meeting of Christian leaders in 431 CE that confirmed Mary's status as the Mother of God.

Eucharist The Christian ceremony that commemorates the Last Supper, in which bread and wine are consumed; also called communion.

excommunication The practice of officially excluding an individual from participating in Christian sacraments.

foederati "The federated"; foreigners allied with the Romans; populated and patrolled land at imperial borders; provided troops for the Roman army.

Golden Horn Inlet of the Bosporus that forms a natural harbor at Constantinople (modern Istanbul).

Goths A German group in the third century CE. Living in Dacia, they were feared plunderers threatening the Roman borders. In the fourth century CE, the West Goths were driven back by the Huns. The Romans allowed them to settle below the Danube River. In 410 CE, they attacked Rome under the leadership of Alaric. The East Goths were conquered by the Huns and moved to Hungary.

Greens Party in Constantinople influential in politics and religion; organized horse races against the Blues party; comprised traders and working-class people.

Hagia Sophia Great domed Church of the Holy Wisdom in Constantinople; designed by Anthemius of Tralles and Isidorus of Miletus; built between 532 and 537 CE under Emperor Justinian.

Huns Central Asiatic people noted for horsemanship and ferocity in battle; drove the Visigoths from Ukraine (ca. 370 CE); conquered eastern and central Europe in the fifth century CE; seized western Europe under Attila (ca. 450 CE).

Illyria Ancient region of the Balkans; part of modern Albania.

Lombards Central European Germanic people; conquered most of Italy in 568 CE, leaving Byzantine rule only on the coast and in the south. The Lombard Empire was subjected by Charlemagne in the eighth century CE.

Lugdunum Roman name for a major city in east-central Gaul; modern Lyon, France.

Manichaeism Religion founded by Mani in Mesopotamia; combines elements of Christianity, Zoroastrianism, Buddhism, and others; postulates two competing principles of good (referred to as light, God, the human soul) and evil (as seen in darkness, the devil, the human body). Mani considered knowledge of light through his teachings and an ascetic way of life as the way to salvation. The Manichaeans were persecuted by Persian kings and Roman emperors.

Mesopotamia Area in western Asia surrounding the Euphrates and Tigris rivers. (The word comes from the Greek meaning "between two rivers.") Floods and irrigation made the land fertile, and around 4500 BCE, the first agricultural settlements were founded there.

Milvian Bridge, Battle of Decisive battle in which Constantine defeated Maxentius in 312 CE.

Monophysitism Fifth-century CE doctrine—from the Greek *monos* (single) and *physis* (nature)—that contended that Jesus Christ had only a single nature, which was divine, not human. That idea conflicted with the orthodox doctrine that Christ was at once human and divine.

Neoplatonism Third-century CE school of Greek philosophy.

Nicaea, Council of Convoked by Constantine I in 325 CE; defined Christian doctrine.

Nicene Creed Statement of faith that is accepted by all Christian churches (eastern Orthodox, western Roman Catholic, and Protestant).

Nika Revolt Uprising (January 13–18, 532 CE) in Constantinople of the Greens and the Blues, who turned the population against Justinian. The population appointed a new emperor and destroyed the city center. Theodora barely prevented Justinian from fleeing. Belisarius repressed the revolt with mercenaries.

Ostrogoths Germanic tribe from Ukraine; subjected by the Huns; migrated to Hungary in the fifth century CE; established a kingdom in Italy under Theodoric (493 CE); defeated under Totila (552 CE).

Parthians Persian horsemen who gained their independence from the Seleucids around 240 BCE and settled in northern Persia; conquered extensive territories to the east of the Seleucid Empire; later fought the Romans.

Picts Ancient people of Great Britain; driven into Scotland by Romans and Britons.

Praetorian Guard Imperial bodyguard in ancient Rome.

Sassanids Dynasty of Persian kings who ruled between 224 and 651 CE; captured Mesopotamia and eastern Syria from the Byzantines in the fourth century CE; conquered Jerusalem in 614 CE; defeated by Alexius in 628 CE.

Severan dynasty Roman dynasty established by Septimius Severus (ruled 197–211 CE); lasted until 235 CE.

Silk Road Ancient overland trade route that extended for 4,000 miles (6,400 km) and linked China and the West. First used as a caravan route, the road ran from Xi'an, China, along the Great Wall, through the Pamir Mountains, into Afghanistan, and on to the eastern Mediterranean Sea, where goods were taken onward by boat, mainly to Rome and Venice. On westbound journeys, the principal cargo was silk; wool, gold, and silver were the main commodities carried in the opposite direction.

Vandals Eastern Germanic people who migrated to Gaul and Spain at the beginning of the fifth century CE; under Gaiseric, founded a kingdom in northern Africa in 429 CE; plundered Rome in 455 CE; defeated by Emperor Justinian I in 534 CE.

Visigoths Germanic people from Ukraine; driven out by the Huns; settled south of the Danube River as foederati (allies) of Rome; rebelled in 378 CE; plundered Rome under Alaric in 410 CE; established a kingdom in Spain conquered by the Arabs in 711 CE

MAJOR HISTORICAL FIGURES

Alaric I King of the Visigoths from around 370 to 410 CE; sacked Rome in 410 CE.

Ambrose, Saint (ca. 340–397 CE) Bishop of Milan; opponent of the Arian heresy.

Anastasius I Byzantine emperor from 491 to 518 CE; supporter of Monophysitism.

Anthony, Saint (ca. 251–356 CE) First Christian monk.

Athanasius, Saint (ca. 293–373 CE) Bishop; opponent of Arianism.

Attila King of the Huns between 434 and 453 CE; conquered western Europe; defeated in Gaul by Romans and Visigoths in 451 CE; plundered Italy in 452 CE.

Augustine of Hippo, Saint (354–430 CE) Christian convert, bishop, theologian, and author of *The City of God*.

Belisarius Sixth-century CE Roman general; conquered the Vandals in Africa in 533–534 CE; defeated the Ostrogoths in Italy in 540 CE.

Benedict of Nursia, Saint (ca. 480–547 CE) Monk from Umbria (Italy); founded Benedictine monastic order.

Bleda (died 445 CE) Nephew of Roas, king of the Huns; along with his brother Attila, succeeded Roas; murdered by Attila.

Cassiodorus (ca. 490–583 CE) Roman statesman and author; stimulated the copying of manuscripts by monks.

Clotilda (474–545 CE) Burgundian wife of Clovis I.

Clovis I King of the Franks between around 481 and 511 CE; conquered most of Gaul; converted in 496 CE.

Constantine Roman emperor between 306 and 337 CE; ruled initially in the west only but became absolute sovereign in 324 CE; built Constantinople; legalized Christianity.

Decius Roman emperor who ruled between 249 and 251 CE. The first systematic persecution of Christians took place during his reign.

Diocletian Roman emperor between 284 and 305 CE.

Domitian Roman emperor who ruled between 81 and 96 CE; presided over a reign of terror.

Gaiseric King of the Vandals between 428 and 477 CE.

Galerius Roman emperor between 305 and 311 CE; persecuted Christians and then issued an edict of tolerance.

Gratian Western Roman emperor between 367 and 383 CE.

Hadrian Roman emperor between 117 and 138 CE.

Honorius Western Roman emperor between 395 and 423 CE; ruled from the age of twelve under the guardianship of Stilicho.

Jerome, Saint (ca. 345–420 CE) Dalmatian-born monastic leader who translated the Bible into Latin.

Julian the Apostate Roman emperor between 361 and 363 CE; converted to paganism and limited the rights of Christians.

Justinian I Byzantine emperor between 527 and 565 CE; built the Hagia Sophia. His generals Belisarius and Narses defeated the Ostrogoths.

Khosrow I King of Persia between 531 and 579 CE.

Mani (ca. 216–276 CE) Persian prophet who founded Manichaeism.

Marcus Aurelius Emperor of Rome between 161 and 180 CE.

Martin of Tours, Saint (ca. 316–397 CE) Bishop of Tours; one of the founders of monasticism.

Narses Sixth-century-CE Roman general of Justinian I; defeated the Ostrogoths in Italy in 552 CE.

Pachomius (ca. 290–346 CE) Founder of monastic commune in Egypt.

Paul of Thebes (ca. 230–341 CE) First Christian hermit; Egyptian who fled persecution by Decius.

Romulus Augustulus Last western Roman emperor; deposed in 476 CE.

Theodora Byzantine empress (ruled 527–548 CE); wife of Justinian I; a Monophysite.

Theodoric the Great
King of the Ostrogoths
between 471 and 526 CE.

Theodosius I Eastern and then
eastern and western Roman
emperor; ruled between 379 and
395 CE.

Valens Eastern Roman emperor;
ruled between 364 and 378 CE.

FOR FURTHER INFORMATION

BOOKS

Bellitto, Christopher M. *The General Councils: A History of the Twenty-one General Councils from Nicaea to Vatican II.* New York: Paulist Press, 2002.

Gibbon, Edward. *The Decline and Fall of the Roman Empire.* New York: Everyman's Library, 2010.

Jackson, L. Charles. *Faith of Our Fathers: A Popular Study of the Nicene Creed.* Moscow, ID: Canon Press, 2007.

Kulikowski, Michael. *Rome's Gothic Wars: From the Third Century to Alaric.* New York: Cambridge University Press, 2008.

Thubron, Colin. *Shadow of the Silk Road.* New York: HarperCollins, 2008.

Wolfram, Herwig (translated by Thomas J. Dunlap). *History of the Goths.* Berkeley, CA: University of California Press, 1990.

WEBSITES

Christianity and the Roman Empire
www.bbc.co.uk/history/ancient/romans/christianityromanempire_article_01.shtml

Ecumenical Councils
www.dailycatholic.org/history/councils.htm

Goths
www.ucalgary.ca/~vandersp/Courses/texts/jordgeti.html

Huns
www.imninalu.net/Huns.htm

Silk Road
www.ess.uci.edu/~oliver/silk.html

Vandals
www.roman-empire.net/articles/article-016.html

marriage, 111
Nika Revolt,
   104–106, 109
Persian peace treaty,
   106–107
Spanish campaign,
   113
Jutes, 95

kampfio, 93
Kathisma, 51
Kavadh I, 107
Khosrow I, 107
knowledge
   preservation,
   91, 99

Leo I, 80, 83, 102
Leo II, 102
Licinius, 36–37, 58
Lombards, 90–96
Longer Rules, 133
Ludovisi Battle
   sarcophagus, 14
Lugdunum, **7**, 17

Macrina, 134
Macrinus, 20
Majorian, 83
Mamaea, Julia, 21
Manichaeism,
   122–124
Marcian, 80–81, 102
Marcus Aurelius, 15
Marmoutier
   monastery, 137

Martin of Tours,
   136–137
martyrdom, 117–118
Mary (Virgin), **116**,
   118–119
Maxentius, 36–37,
   57–58
Maximian, 34–35, **34**
Maximinus, 22–24
Maximus, Magnus,
   42
Meroë, **7**, **9**, 11
Merovingian dynasty,
   84
Mese, 50
Mesopotamia, **7**, 8–9,
   18, 20, 22
monasteries, 91, 99
monasticism
   abbot's authority,
      133–134, 139
   appeal of, 130–132
   cenobitic (monastic)
      rules, 132
   dissension, 133–134
   Eastern, 133–134
   living arrangements,
      134, 140
   ora et labora (prayer
      and work), 134,
      140
   organized, 132
   overview, 135
   Western, 136–137
Monophysitism,
   53–54, 106

Narses, 112
Neoplatonism,
   123–124
Nepos, Julius, 77
Nero, 117
Nestorius, 118
Nicaea, 53, 59
Nicene Creed, 60
Niger, Pescennius, 17,
   45
Nika Revolt,
   104–106, 109
novitiate (trial
   period), 132
Nubians, Nubian
   Empire, 10–11
Numerian, 33

Odaenathus, 26–27
Odoacer, 77, 102
ora et labora
   (prayer and work),
   134, 140
Orestes, 77
Ostrogoths, 55,
   71–72, 76–79, 102,
   110
Ottomans, 109

Pachomius, 132
paganism, 62–67, 130
Palestine, 27
Palmyra, 7, 25–27
Papinian, 18
Parthians, 7, 8–9, 13,
   18, 20